# 70+ Homema
# Coffee Creamer Recipes

Featuring the full coffee creamer series made by

# Table of Contents

70+ Flavored Coffee Creamer Recipes

# Table of Contents

Flavored Coffee Creamer Recipes

# Table of Contents

### Flavored Coffee Creamer Recipes

## My Own Recipes

# Frequently Asked Questions

**Q: Why is it recommended to heat up homemade coffee creamer?**
*A: The heating process allows the alcohol from the extracts to evaporate leaving you with a smoother tasting creamer. It also allows the ingredients to mix better. Do NOT let it boil. You should be able to stick your finger in without burning yourself.*

**Q: A lot of these recipes use sweetened condensed milk, does that mean they're crazy high in sugar?**
*A: No, not at all! These homemade coffee creamers have less sugar, carbs, and calories than most store bought creamers. It's important to remember that sweetened condensed milk is just one ingredient in the recipe. You are diluting it with 2+ cups of milk. Once diluted, most of these recipes are around 3.5g of sugar per tbsp compared to 5g-8g of sugar per tbsp with most store bought creamers.*

*You can find nutritional fact calculators online to determine your exact nutritional facts based on the exact ingredients that you use. When comparing to store bought creamers, the recommended serving size is 1 tablespoon. This is the same serving size that store bought creamers recommend. When comparing to store bought nutritional facts, you must use the same serving size for an accurate comparison.*

**Q: Can I use bakery emulsions instead of extracts?**
*A: Yes! 1 teaspoon extract = 1 teaspoon emulsion*
*Bakery emulsions are a great alternative to extracts. If a recipe calls for 1 teaspoon of extract, substitute with 1 teaspoon of emulsion.*

**Q: Can I use coffee syrups instead of extracts or emulsions?**
*A: Yes! 1 teaspoon extract = 1-2 tablespoon coffee syrup*
*Coffee syrups are not as strong as extracts so you'll need to use more. If a recipe calls for 1 teaspoon of extract or emulsion, use 1-2 tablespoon of coffee syrups instead, depending on how strong it is.*

**Q: How can I make these recipes dairy free or sugar free?**
*A: For your milk of choice, choose a dairy free milk alternative. Substitute the sweetened condensed milk with sweetened condensed coconut milk OR sweetened condensed oat milk. Each recipe has dairy free and sugar substitutions listed.*

**Q: Why is my coffee creamer so thick / gel like after it cools?**
*A: This usually happens when your mixture was not properly mixed or it got too hot. It is recommended to heat the coffee creamers to allow that alcohol from the extracts to evaporate. That happens right at steaming temperature. As soon as it starts steaming, remove it from heat immediately. Do not let it boil. You should be able to stick your finger in it without burning yourself. If you can't do that, it's too hot and it will start to condense again. This is why it thickens as it cools.*

**CONTAINER SIZE:** 1 Quart (32 oz)

**MY RATING:** ☆☆☆☆☆

## INGREDIENTS

- 14 oz. sweetened condensed milk
- 2 cups milk of choice
- 1-2 tsp. almond extract
  - OR 2-4 tbsp. almond syrup
- 1/2 tsp. cherry extract or cherry emulsion
  - OR 1 tbsp. cherry syrup
- 1 tsp. vanilla extract
  - OR 2 tbsp. vanilla syrup

## DIRECTIONS

Combine all ingredients and mix well. Warm over medium heat for a few minutes until your mixture just starts to steam. Once it starts steaming, remove it from heat. Let it cool then transfer to your container.

## SUGAR FREE VERSION

- 3 cups milk of choice
- 1 cup sugar free amaretto syrup
  - OR 3/4 cup sugar free almond syrup
  - + 1/4 cup sugar free cherry syrup

*Put in your container and shake. No need to heat.*

## DAIRY FREE VERSION

Follow instructions above but use these substitutions:
- 1 can sweetened condensed coconut milk OR sweetened condensed oat milk
- 2 1/4 cups milk alternative of choice (or more as needed)

## EXPIRATION DATE

Use the expiration date listed on the milk or milk substitute that you used.

## MY NOTES

*Amaretto Coffee Creamer*

*NUTRITIONAL FACTS: Homemade coffee creamer has less sugar, carbs, and calories than most store bought creamers. You can find nutritional fact calculators online to determine your exact nutritional facts based on the exact ingredients that you use. When comparing to store bought creamers, the recommended serving size is 1 tablespoon. This is the same serving size that store bought creamers recommend.*

**CONTAINER SIZE:** 1 Quart (32 oz)

**MY RATING:** ☆☆☆☆☆

## INGREDIENTS

- 14 oz. sweetened condensed milk
- 2 cups milk of choice
- 2 tsp. banana extract
    - OR 4 tbsp. banana syrup
- 1 tsp. vanilla extract
    - OR 1 tbsp. vanilla syrup

## DIRECTIONS

Combine all ingredients and mix well. Warm over medium heat for a few minutes until your mixture just starts to steam. Once it starts steaming, remove it from heat. Let it cool then transfer to your container.

## SUGAR FREE VERSION

- 3 cups milk of choice
- 2/3 cup sugar free banana syrup
- 1/3 cup sugar free vanilla syrup

*Put in your container and shake. No need to heat.*

## DAIRY FREE VERSION

Follow instructions above but use these substitutions:
- 1 can sweetened condensed coconut milk OR sweetened condensed oat milk
- 2 1/4 cups milk alternative of choice (or more as needed)

## EXPIRATION DATE

Use the expiration date listed on the milk or milk substitute that you used.

## NOTES

*Banana Cream Pie Coffee Creamer*

*NUTRITIONAL FACTS: Homemade coffee creamer has less sugar, carbs, and calories than most store bought creamers. You can find nutritional fact calculators online to determine your exact nutritional facts based on the exact ingredients that you use. When comparing to store bought creamers, the recommended serving size is 1 tablespoon. This is the same serving size that store bought creamers recommend.*

# Banana Nut Bread

**CONTAINER SIZE:** 1 Quart (32 oz)

**MY RATING:** ☆☆☆☆☆

## INGREDIENTS

- 14 oz. sweetened condensed milk
- 2 cups milk of choice
- 1 tbsp. brown sugar
- 1 -2 tsp. banana extract
    - OR 3 tbsp. banana syrup
- 1 tsp. vanilla extract
    - OR 2 tbsp. vanilla syrup
- 1 tsp. hazelnut extract or emulsion
    - OR 2 tbsp. hazelnut syrup

## DIRECTIONS

Combine all ingredients and mix well. Warm over medium heat for a few minutes until your mixture just starts to steam. Once it starts steaming, remove it from heat. Let it cool then transfer to your container.

## SUGAR FREE VERSION

- 3 cups milk of choice
- 1/2 cup sugar free banana syrup
- 1/4 cup sugar free vanilla syrup
- 1 /4 cup sugar free hazelnut syrup

*Put in your container and shake. No need to heat.*

## DAIRY FREE VERSION

Follow instructions above but use these substitutions:
- 1 can sweetened condensed coconut milk OR sweetened condensed oat milk
- 2 1/4 cups milk alternative of choice (or more as needed)

## EXPIRATION DATE

Use the expiration date listed on the milk or milk substitute that you used.

## NOTES

*Banana Nut Bread Coffee Creamer*

*NUTRITIONAL FACTS: Homemade coffee creamer has less sugar, carbs, and calories than most store bought creamers. You can find nutritional fact calculators online to determine your exact nutritional facts based on the exact ingredients that you use. When comparing to store bought creamers, the recommended serving size is 1 tablespoon. This is the same serving size that store bought creamers recommend.*

**Bananas Foster**

**CONTAINER SIZE:** 1 Quart (32 oz)

**MY RATING:** ☆☆☆☆☆

## INGREDIENTS

- 14 oz. sweetened condensed milk
- 2 cups milk of choice
- 1 tbsp. brown sugar
- 1 tsp banana extract
- 1 tsp. rum extract
- 1 tsp. vanilla extract
- 1 tsp. butter extract
- 1/2 tsp cinnamon extract
  - OR 1 tsp ground cinnamon

## DIRECTIONS

Combine sweetened condensed milk and cinnamon and mix well. Then mix in all other ingredients. Warm over medium heat for a few minutes until your mixture just starts to steam. Once it starts steaming, remove it from heat. Let it cool then transfer to your container.

## SUGAR FREE VERSION

Make your own sweetened condensed milk using a sugar alternative such as monk fruit or stevia. Check out page 70 for tips on how to make your own!

There are tons of recipes online for homemade sweetened condensed milk using just about every kind of sugar substitute available too! Just make sure to read the reviews first!

## DAIRY FREE VERSION

Follow instructions above but use these substitutions:
- 1 can sweetened condensed coconut milk OR sweetened condensed oat milk
- 2 1/4 cups milk alternative of choice (or more as needed)

## EXPIRATION DATE

Use the expiration date listed on the milk or milk substitute that you used.

## NOTES

*Bananas Foster Coffee Creamer*

*NUTRITIONAL FACTS: Homemade coffee creamer has less sugar, carbs, and calories than most store bought creamers. You can find nutritional fact calculators online to determine your exact nutritional facts based on the exact ingredients that you use. When comparing to store bought creamers, the recommended serving size is 1 tablespoon. This is the same serving size that store bought creamers recommend.*

**Berries & Cream**

**CONTAINER SIZE:** 1 Quart (32 oz)

**MY RATING:** ☆ ☆ ☆ ☆ ☆

## INGREDIENTS

- 14 oz. sweetened condensed milk
- 2 cups milk of choice
- 1 tsp. vanilla extract
    - OR 1 tbsp. vanilla syrup
- 1 tsp. strawberry emulsion
    - OR 1 tbsp. strawberry syrup
- 1/2 tsp. blueberry emulsion
    - OR 1/2 tbsp. blueberry syrup

## DIRECTIONS

Combine all ingredients and mix well. Warm over medium heat for a few minutes until your mixture just starts to steam. Once it starts steaming, remove it from heat. Let it cool then transfer to your container.

## SUGAR FREE VERSION

- 3 cups milk of choice
- 2/3 cup sugar free strawberry syrup
- 1/3 cup sugar free blueberry syrup

*Put in your container and shake. No need to heat.*

## DAIRY FREE VERSION

Follow instructions above but use these substitutions:
- 1 can sweetened condensed coconut milk OR sweetened condensed oat milk
- 2 1/4 cups milk alternative of choice (or more as needed)

## EXPIRATION DATE

Use the expiration date listed on the milk or milk substitute that you used.

## NOTES

*Berries & Cream Coffee Creamer*

*NUTRITIONAL FACTS: Homemade coffee creamer has less sugar, carbs, and calories than most store bought creamers. You can find nutritional fact calculators online to determine your exact nutritional facts based on the exact ingredients that you use. When comparing to store bought creamers, the recommended serving size is 1 tablespoon. This is the same serving size that store bought creamers recommend.*

**Blueberry Muffin**

CONTAINER SIZE: 1 Quart (32 oz)

MY RATING: ☆☆☆☆☆

## INGREDIENTS

- 14 oz. sweetened condensed milk
- 2 cups buttermilk
  - (hack: 2 cups milk + 2 tbsp. lemon juice or vinegar)
- 2 tsp. vanilla extract
  - OR 2 tbsp. vanilla syrup
- 1 tsp. blueberry emulsion
  - OR 1 tbsp. blueberry syrup

## DIRECTIONS

Combine all ingredients and mix well. Warm over medium heat for a few minutes until your mixture just starts to steam. Once it starts steaming, remove it from heat. Let it cool then transfer to your container.

## SUGAR FREE VERSION

- 3 cups milk of choice
- 3/4 cup sugar free blueberry syrup
- 1/4 cup sugar free vanilla syrup

*Put in your container and shake. No need to heat.*

## DAIRY FREE VERSION

Follow instructions above but use these substitutions:
- 1 can sweetened condensed coconut milk OR sweetened condensed oat milk
- 2 1/4 cups milk alternative of choice (or more as needed)

## EXPIRATION DATE

Use the expiration date listed on the milk or milk substitute that you used.

## NOTES

*Blueberry Muffin Coffee Creamer*

*NUTRITIONAL FACTS: Homemade coffee creamer has less sugar, carbs, and calories than most store bought creamers. You can find nutritional fact calculators online to determine your exact nutritional facts based on the exact ingredients that you use. When comparing to store bought creamers, the recommended serving size is 1 tablespoon. This is the same serving size that store bought creamers recommend.*

# Brown Butter Chocolate Chip

**CONTAINER SIZE:** 1 Quart                                    **MY RATING:** ☆☆☆☆☆

## INGREDIENTS

- 14 oz. sweetened condensed milk
- 2 cups milk of choice
- 2 tsp. vanilla extract
    - OR 2 tbsp. vanilla syrup
- 1 tbsp. unsweetened cocoa powder
- 2 tbsp. brown sugar
- 1 tbsp. butter
    - OR 1 tsp. butter extract

## DIRECTIONS

Combine brown sugar and butter, heat until bubbling. Then add in all other ingredients, mix well. Warm over medium heat for a few minutes until your mixture just starts to steam. Once it starts steaming, remove it from heat. Let it cool then transfer to your container.

*It is normal for ground spices to settle during storage. Just give it a quick shake before each use. If you prefer no settling spices, you can strain your mixture through a cheesecloth to filter out the spices as you put it in your container.*

## SUGAR FREE VERSION

- 3 cups milk of choice
- 1 cup sugar free chocolate chip cookie syrup

*Put in your container and shake. No need to heat.*

## DAIRY FREE VERSION

Follow instructions above but use these substitutions:
- 1 can sweetened condensed coconut milk OR sweetened condensed oat milk
- 2 1/4 cups milk alternative of choice (or more as needed)

## EXPIRATION DATE

Use the expiration date listed on the milk or milk substitute that you used.

## NOTES

*Brown Butter Chocolate Chip Cookie Coffee Creamer*

*NUTRITIONAL FACTS: Homemade coffee creamer has less sugar, carbs, and calories than most store bought creamers. You can find nutritional fact calculators online to determine your exact nutritional facts based on the exact ingredients that you use. When comparing to store bought creamers, the recommended serving size is 1 tablespoon. This is the same serving size that store bought creamers recommend.*

**CONTAINER SIZE:** 1 Quart (32 oz)

**MY RATING:** ☆☆☆☆☆

## INGREDIENTS

- 14 oz. sweetened condensed milk
- 2 cups milk of choice
- 1 tbsp. light brown sugar
- 2 tsp. vanilla extract
    - OR 4 tbsp. vanilla syrup
- 2 tsp. cake batter extract or emulsion
    - OR 4 tbsp. birthday cake syrup

## DIRECTIONS

Combine all ingredients and mix well. Warm over medium heat for a few minutes until your mixture just starts to steam. Once it starts steaming, remove it from heat. Let it cool then transfer to your container.

## SUGAR FREE VERSION

- 3 cups milk of choice
- 1/4 cup sugar free vanilla syrup
- 1/4 cup sugar free brown sugar syrup
- 1/2 cup sugar free birthday cake syrup

*Put in your container and shake. No need to heat.*

## DAIRY FREE VERSION

Follow instructions above but use these substitutions:
- 1 can sweetened condensed coconut milk OR sweetened condensed oat milk
- 2 1/4 cups milk alternative of choice (or more as needed)

## EXPIRATION DATE

Use the expiration date listed on the milk or milk substitute that you used.

## NOTES

*Cake Batter Coffee Creamer*

*NUTRITIONAL FACTS: Homemade coffee creamer has less sugar, carbs, and calories than most store bought creamers. You can find nutritional fact calculators online to determine your exact nutritional facts based on the exact ingredients that you use. When comparing to store bought creamers, the recommended serving size is 1 tablespoon. This is the same serving size that store bought creamers recommend.*

**CONTAINER SIZE:** 1 Quart (32 oz)

MY RATING: ☆☆☆☆☆

*"Popular Candy Bar Flavor"*

## INGREDIENTS

- 14 oz. sweetened condensed milk
- 2 cups milk of choice
- 1 tsp. vanilla extract
  - OR 2 tbsp. vanilla syrup
- 3 tbsp. caramel sauce or syrup
- 1 tsp. cookie butter emulsion
- 2 tbsp. unsweetened cocoa powder

## DIRECTIONS

Combine sweetened condensed milk and cocoa powder first. Mix well then mix in all other ingredients. Warm over medium heat for a few minutes until your mixture just starts to steam. Once it starts steaming, remove it from heat. Let it cool then transfer to your container.

*It is normal for ground spices to settle during storage. Just give it a quick shake before each use. If you prefer no settling spices, you can strain your mixture through a cheesecloth to filter out the spices as you put it in your container.*

## SUGAR FREE VERSION

- 3 cups milk of choice
- 1/4 cup sugar free mocha syrup
- 1/4 cup sugar free cookie syrup
- 1/2 cup sugar free caramel syrup

*Put in your container and shake. No need to heat.*

## DAIRY FREE VERSION

Follow instructions above but use these substitutions:
- 1 can sweetened condensed coconut milk OR sweetened condensed oat milk
- 2 1/4 cups milk alternative of choice (or more as needed)

## EXPIRATION DATE

Use the expiration date listed on the milk or milk substitute that you used.

## NOTES

*Caramel & Cookie Bar Coffee Creamer*

*NUTRITIONAL FACTS: Homemade coffee creamer has less sugar, carbs, and calories than most store bought creamers. You can find nutritional fact calculators online to determine your exact nutritional facts based on the exact ingredients that you use. When comparing to store bought creamers, the recommended serving size is 1 tablespoon. This is the same serving size that store bought creamers recommend.*

**Caramel Apple**

CONTAINER SIZE: 1 Quart (32 oz)

MY RATING: ☆ ☆ ☆ ☆ ☆

## INGREDIENTS

- 14 oz. sweetened condensed milk
- 2 cups milk of choice
- 1 tsp. vanilla extract
  - OR 1 tbsp. vanilla syrup
- 3 tbsp. caramel sauce or syrup of choice
- 1 tsp. green apple emulsion or extract

## DIRECTIONS

Combine all ingredients and mix well. Warm over medium heat for a few minutes until your mixture just starts to steam. Once it starts steaming, remove it from heat. Let it cool then transfer to your container.

## SUGAR FREE VERSION

- 3 cups milk of choice
- 1 cup sugar free caramel apple syrup
  - OR 1/2 cup sugar free apple syrup
  - +1/2 cup sugar free caramel syrup

*Put in your container and shake. No need to heat.*

## DAIRY FREE VERSION

Follow instructions above but use these substitutions:
- 1 can sweetened condensed coconut milk OR sweetened condensed oat milk
- 2 1/4 cups milk alternative of choice (or more as needed)

## EXPIRATION DATE

Use the expiration date listed on the milk or milk substitute that you used.

## NOTES

*Caramel Apple Coffee Creamer*

*NUTRITIONAL FACTS: Homemade coffee creamer has less sugar, carbs, and calories than most store bought creamers. You can find nutritional fact calculators online to determine your exact nutritional facts based on the exact ingredients that you use. When comparing to store bought creamers, the recommended serving size is 1 tablespoon. This is the same serving size that store bought creamers recommend.*

# Caramel Macchiato

**CONTAINER SIZE:** 1 Quart (32 oz)

**MY RATING:** ☆☆☆☆☆

## INGREDIENTS

- 14 oz. sweetened condensed milk
- 2 cups milk of choice
- 1 tsp. espresso powder
    - OR 2-3 tsp. instant coffee powder
- 1/3 cup caramel sauce or syrup
- 2 tsp. vanilla extract
    - OR 4 tbsp. vanilla syrup

## DIRECTIONS

Combine sweetened condensed milk and espresso powder first. Mix well then mix in all other ingredients. Warm over medium heat for a few minutes until your mixture just starts to steam. Once it starts steaming, remove it from heat. Let it cool then transfer to your container.

## SUGAR FREE VERSION

- 3 cups milk of choice
- 1 cup sugar free caramel macchiato syrup
    - OR 1 cup sugar free caramel syrup
    - +1 tsp. espresso powder

*Put in your container and shake. Mix well! No need to heat.*

## DAIRY FREE VERSION

Follow instructions above but use these substitutions:
- 1 can sweetened condensed coconut milk OR sweetened condensed oat milk
- 2 1/4 cups milk alternative of choice (or more as needed)

## EXPIRATION DATE

Use the expiration date listed on the milk or milk substitute that you used.

## NOTES

*Caramel Macchiato Coffee Creamer*

*NUTRITIONAL FACTS: Homemade coffee creamer has less sugar, carbs, and calories than most store bought creamers. You can find nutritional fact calculators online to determine your exact nutritional facts based on the exact ingredients that you use. When comparing to store bought creamers, the recommended serving size is 1 tablespoon. This is the same serving size that store bought creamers recommend.*

**CONTAINER SIZE:** 1 Quart (32 oz)

**MY RATING:** ☆☆☆☆☆

## INGREDIENTS

- 1/4 cup pecans + 1 cup thin milk (blended)
- 14 oz. sweetened condensed milk
- 1 cup milk of choice
- 1 tsp. vanilla extract
    - OR 1 tbsp. vanilla syrup
- 1/4 cup caramel sauce or syrup of your choice

## DIRECTIONS

Blend 1/4 cup pecans and 1 cup of 2% milk together until well blended. Using a fine mesh strainer, strain the pecan milk mixture as you pour it into the pan. Add in the rest of the ingredients. Warm over medium heat for a few minutes until your mixture just starts to steam. Once it starts steaming, remove it from heat. Let it cool then transfer to your container.

## SUGAR FREE VERSION

- 3 cups milk of choice
- 1 cup sugar free caramel pecan syrup
    - OR 1/2 cup sugar free caramel syrup
    - +1/2 cup sugar free pecan syrup

*Put in your container and shake. No need to heat.*

## DAIRY FREE VERSION

Follow instructions above but use these substitutions:
- 1 can sweetened condensed coconut milk OR sweetened condensed oat milk
- 2 1/4 cups milk alternative of choice (or more as needed)

## EXPIRATION DATE

Use the expiration date listed on the milk or milk substitute that you used.

## NOTES

*Caramel Pecan Coffee Creamer*

*NUTRITIONAL FACTS: Homemade coffee creamer has less sugar, carbs, and calories than most store bought creamers. You can find nutritional fact calculators online to determine your exact nutritional facts based on the exact ingredients that you use. When comparing to store bought creamers, the recommended serving size is 1 tablespoon. This is the same serving size that store bought creamers recommend.*

# Chocolate & Hazelnut

**CONTAINER SIZE:** 1 Quart (32 oz)

**MY RATING:** ☆☆☆☆☆

*"Popular Chocolate Candy covered with hazelnuts"*

## INGREDIENTS

- 14 oz. sweetened condensed milk
- 2 cups milk of choice
- 1 tsp. vanilla extract
    - OR 1 tbsp. vanilla syrup
- 2 tbsp. unsweetened cocoa powder
    - OR 4 tbsp. mocha syrup
- 3 tsp. hazelnut extract
    - OR 3 tbsp. hazelnut syrup

## DIRECTIONS

Combine sweetened condensed milk and cocoa powder first. Mix well then mix in all other ingredients. Warm over medium heat for a few minutes until your mixture just starts to steam. Once it starts steaming, remove it from heat. Let it cool then transfer to your container.

*It is normal for ground spices to settle during storage. Just give it a quick shake before each use. If you prefer no settling spices, you can strain your mixture through a cheesecloth to filter out the spices as you put it in your container.*

## SUGAR FREE VERSION

- 3 cups milk of choice
- 3/4 cup sugar free mocha syrup
- 1/4 cup sugar free hazelnut syrup

*Put in your container and shake. No need to heat.*

## DAIRY FREE VERSION

Follow instructions above but use these substitutions:
- 1 can sweetened condensed coconut milk OR sweetened condensed oat milk
- 2 1/4 cups milk alternative of choice (or more as needed)

## EXPIRATION DATE

Use the expiration date listed on the milk or milk substitute that you used.

## NOTES

*Chocolate & Hazelnut Coffee Creamer*

*NUTRITIONAL FACTS: Homemade coffee creamer has less sugar, carbs, and calories than most store bought creamers. You can find nutritional fact calculators online to determine your exact nutritional facts based on the exact ingredients that you use. When comparing to store bought creamers, the recommended serving size is 1 tablespoon. This is the same serving size that store bought creamers recommend.*

**Chocolate Caramel Coconut Cookie**

**CONTAINER SIZE:** 1 Quart (32 oz)

**MY RATING:** ☆☆☆☆☆

*"Popular Cookie Flavor"*

## INGREDIENTS

- 14 oz. sweetened condensed milk
- 2 cups milk of choice
- 2 tbsp. unsweetened cocoa powder
- 2 tbsp. caramel sauce or syrup
- 2 tsp. coconut extract or emulsion
    - OR 4 tbsp. coconut syrup
- 1 tsp. vanilla extract
    - OR 1 tbsp. vanilla syrup

## DIRECTIONS

Combine sweetened condensed milk and unsweetened cocoa powder first. Mix well then add in all other ingredients and mix well. Warm over medium heat for a few minutes until your mixture just starts to steam. Once it starts steaming, remove it from heat. Let it cool then transfer to your container.

*It is normal for ground spices to settle during storage. Just give it a quick shake before each use. If you prefer no settling spices, you can strain your mixture through a cheesecloth to filter out the spices as you put it in your container*

## SUGAR FREE VERSION

- 3 cups milk of choice
- 1/3 cup sugar free caramel syrup
- 1/4 cup sugar free mocha syrup
- 3 tbsp. sugar free coconut syrup

*Put in your container and shake. No need to heat.*

## DAIRY FREE VERSION

Follow instructions above but use these substitutions:
- 1 can sweetened condensed coconut milk OR sweetened condensed oat milk
- 2 1/4 cups milk alternative of choice (or more as needed)

## EXPIRATION DATE

Use the expiration date listed on the milk or milk substitute that you used.

## NOTES

*Chocolate Caramel Coconut Cookie Coffee Creamer*

*NUTRITIONAL FACTS: Homemade coffee creamer has less sugar, carbs, and calories than most store bought creamers. You can find nutritional fact calculators online to determine your exact nutritional facts based on the exact ingredients that you use. When comparing to store bought creamers, the recommended serving size is 1 tablespoon. This is the same serving size that store bought creamers recommend.*

**CONTAINER SIZE:** 1 Quart (32 oz)

**MY RATING:** ☆☆☆☆☆

## INGREDIENTS

- 14 oz. sweetened condensed milk
- 2 cups milk of choice
- 1 tsp. vanilla extract
    - OR 2 tbsp. vanilla syrup
- 1/4 cup caramel sauce or syrup
- 1/4 cup unsweetened cocoa powder

## DIRECTIONS

Combine sweetened condensed milk and cocoa powder first. Mix well then mix in all other ingredients. Warm over medium heat for a few minutes until your mixture just starts to steam. Once it starts steaming, remove it from heat. Let it cool then transfer to your container.

*It is normal for ground spices to settle during storage. Just give it a quick shake before each use. If you prefer no settling spices, you can strain your mixture through a cheesecloth to filter out the spices as you put it in your container.*

## SUGAR FREE VERSION

- 3 cups milk of choice
- 1/2 cup sugar free mocha syrup
- 1/2 cup sugar free caramel syrup

*Put in your container and shake. No need to heat.*

## DAIRY FREE VERSION

Follow instructions above but use these substitutions:

- 1 can sweetened condensed coconut milk OR sweetened condensed oat milk
- 2 1/4 cups milk alternative of choice (or more as needed)

## EXPIRATION DATE

Use the expiration date listed on the milk or milk substitute that you used.

## NOTES

*Chocolate Caramel Coffee Creamer*

*NUTRITIONAL FACTS: Homemade coffee creamer has less sugar, carbs, and calories than most store bought creamers. You can find nutritional fact calculators online to determine your exact nutritional facts based on the exact ingredients that you use. When comparing to store bought creamers, the recommended serving size is 1 tablespoon. This is the same serving size that store bought creamers recommend.*

# Chocolate Covered Cherries

**MY RATING:** ☆☆☆☆☆

## INGREDIENTS

- 14 oz. sweetened condensed milk
- 3 tbsp. unsweetened cocoa powder
- 2 cups milk of choice
- 1 tsp. vanilla extract
    - OR 1 tbsp. vanilla syrup
- 1 tsp. cherry emulsion
    - OR 1 tbsp. cherry syrup

## DIRECTIONS

Combine sweetened condensed milk and cocoa powder together first, mix well. Then add in all other ingredients. Warm over medium heat for a few minutes until your mixture just starts to steam. Once it starts steaming, remove it from heat. Let it cool then transfer to your container.

*It is normal for ground spices to settle during storage. Just give it a quick shake before each use. If you prefer no settling spices, you can strain your mixture through a cheesecloth to filter out the spices as you put it in your container.*

## SUGAR FREE VERSION

- 3 cups milk of choice
- 3/4 cup sugar free mocha syrup
- 1/4 cup sugar free cherry syrup

*Put in your container and shake. No need to heat.*

## DAIRY FREE VERSION

Follow instructions above but use these substitutions:
- 1 can sweetened condensed coconut milk OR sweetened condensed oat milk
- 2 1/4 cups milk alternative of choice (or more as needed)

## EXPIRATION DATE

Use the expiration date listed on the milk or milk substitute that you used.

## NOTES

*Chocolate Covered Cherries Coffee Creamer*

*NUTRITIONAL FACTS: Homemade coffee creamer has less sugar, carbs, and calories than most store bought creamers. You can find nutritional fact calculators online to determine your exact nutritional facts based on the exact ingredients that you use. When comparing to store bought creamers, the recommended serving size is 1 tablespoon. This is the same serving size that store bought creamers recommend.*

# Chocolate Covered Strawberries

**CONTAINER SIZE:** 1 Quart (32 oz)

**MY RATING:** ☆☆☆☆☆

## INGREDIENTS

- 14 oz. sweetened condensed milk
- 2 cups milk of choice
- 2 tsp. vanilla extract
    - OR 2 tbsp. vanilla syrup
- 2 tsp. strawberry extract
    - OR 2 tbsp. strawberry syrup
- 2 tbsp. unsweetened cocoa powder

## DIRECTIONS

Combine sweetened condensed milk and cocoa powder first. Mix well then mix in all other ingredients. Warm over medium heat for a few minutes until your mixture just starts to steam. Once it starts steaming, remove it from heat. Let it cool then transfer to your container.

*It is normal for ground spices to settle during storage. Just give it a quick shake before each use. If you prefer no settling spices, you can strain your mixture through a cheesecloth to filter out the spices as you put it in your container.*

## SUGAR FREE VERSION

- 3 cups milk of choice
- 3/4 cup sugar free mocha syrup
- 1/4 cup sugar free strawberry syrup

*Put in your container and shake. No need to heat.*

## DAIRY FREE VERSION

Follow instructions above but use these substitutions:
- 1 can sweetened condensed coconut milk OR sweetened condensed oat milk
- 2 1/4 cups milk alternative of choice (or more as needed)

## EXPIRATION DATE

Use the expiration date listed on the milk or milk substitute that you used.

## NOTES

Chocolate Covered Strawberries Coffee Creamer

*NUTRITIONAL FACTS: Homemade coffee creamer has less sugar, carbs, and calories than most store bought creamers. You can find nutritional fact calculators online to determine your exact nutritional facts based on the exact ingredients that you use. When comparing to store bought creamers, the recommended serving size is 1 tablespoon. This is the same serving size that store bought creamers recommend.*

**Cinnamon Churro**

**CONTAINER SIZE:** 1 Quart (32 oz)

**MY RATING:** ☆☆☆☆☆

## INGREDIENTS

- 14 oz. sweetened condensed milk
- 2 cups milk of choice
- 1 tbsp. vanilla extract
  - OR 3 tbsp. vanilla syrup
- 1 tsp. ground cinnamon
  - OR 2 tsp. cinnamon extract
- 1 tbsp. brown sugar

## DIRECTIONS

Combine sweetened condensed milk and cinnamon first. Mix well then mix in all other ingredients. Warm over medium heat for a few minutes until your mixture just starts to steam. Once it starts steaming, remove it from heat. Let it cool then transfer to your container.

*It is normal for ground spices to settle during storage. Just give it a quick shake before each use. If you prefer no settling spices, you can strain your mixture through a cheesecloth to filter out the spices as you put it in your container.*

## SUGAR FREE VERSION

- 3 cups milk of choice
- 1 cup sugar free churro syrup

*Put in your container and shake. No need to heat.*

## DAIRY FREE VERSION

Follow instructions above but use these substitutions:
- 1 can sweetened condensed coconut milk OR sweetened condensed oat milk
- 2 1/4 cups milk alternative of choice (or more as needed)

## EXPIRATION DATE

Use the expiration date listed on the milk or milk substitute that you used.

## NOTES

*Cinnamon Churro Coffee Creamer*

*NUTRITIONAL FACTS: Homemade coffee creamer has less sugar, carbs, and calories than most store bought creamers. You can find nutritional fact calculators online to determine your exact nutritional facts based on the exact ingredients that you use. When comparing to store bought creamers, the recommended serving size is 1 tablespoon. This is the same serving size that store bought creamers recommend.*

**CONTAINER SIZE:** 1 Quart (32 oz)

**MY RATING:** ☆☆☆☆☆

## INGREDIENTS

- 14 oz. sweetened condensed milk
- 2 cups milk of choice
- 1 tsp. ground cinnamon
    - OR 1 tsp. cinnamon extract
- 1/2 tsp. vanilla extract
    - OR 1/2 tbsp. vanilla syrup
- 5 oz. caramel sauce or syrup

## DIRECTIONS

Combine sweetened condensed milk, caramel and cinnamon first. Mix well then mix in all other ingredients. Warm over medium heat for a few minutes until your mixture just starts to steam. Once it starts steaming, remove it from heat. Let it cool then transfer to your container.

*It is normal for ground spices to settle during storage. Just give it a quick shake before each use. If you prefer no settling spices, you can strain your mixture through a cheesecloth to filter out the spices as you put it in your container.*

## SUGAR FREE VERSION

- 3 cups milk of choice
- 1 cup sugar free cinnamon dolce syrup

*Put in your container and shake. No need to heat.*

## DAIRY FREE VERSION

Follow instructions above but use these substitutions:
- 1 can sweetened condensed coconut milk OR sweetened condensed oat milk
- 2 1/4 cups milk alternative of choice (or more as needed)

## EXPIRATION DATE

Use the expiration date listed on the milk or milk substitute that you used.

## NOTES

*Cinnamon Dolce Coffee Creamer*

*NUTRITIONAL FACTS: Homemade coffee creamer has less sugar, carbs, and calories than most store bought creamers. You can find nutritional fact calculators online to determine your exact nutritional facts based on the exact ingredients that you use. When comparing to store bought creamers, the recommended serving size is 1 tablespoon. This is the same serving size that store bought creamers recommend.*

# Cinnamon Hazelnut

**CONTAINER SIZE:** 1 Quart (32 oz)

**MY RATING:** ☆☆☆☆☆

## INGREDIENTS

- 14 oz. sweetened condensed milk
- 2 cups milk of choice
- 2 tsp. ground cinnamon
    - OR 1 tsp. cinnamon extract
- 1 tsp. hazelnut emulsion or extract
    - OR 1-2 tbsp. hazelnut syrup
- 1 tsp. vanilla extract
    - OR 1 tbsp. vanilla syrup

## DIRECTIONS

Combine sweetened condensed milk and cinnamon first. Mix well then mix in all other ingredients. Warm over medium heat for a few minutes until your mixture just starts to steam. Once it starts steaming, remove it from heat. Let it cool then transfer to your container.

*It is normal for ground spices to settle during storage. Just give it a quick shake before each use. If you prefer no settling spices, you can strain your mixture through a cheesecloth to filter out the spices as you put it in your container.*

## SUGAR FREE VERSION

- 3 cups milk of choice
- 3/4 cup sugar free hazelnut syrup
- 1/4 cup sugar free cinnamon syrup

*Put in your container and shake. No need to heat.*

## DAIRY FREE VERSION

Follow instructions above but use these substitutions:
- 1 can sweetened condensed coconut milk OR sweetened condensed oat milk
- 2 1/4 cups milk alternative of choice (or more as needed)

## EXPIRATION DATE

Use the expiration date listed on the milk or milk substitute that you used.

## NOTES

*Cinnamon Hazelnut Coffee Creamer*

*NUTRITIONAL FACTS: Homemade coffee creamer has less sugar, carbs, and calories than most store bought creamers. You can find nutritional fact calculators online to determine your exact nutritional facts based on the exact ingredients that you use. When comparing to store bought creamers, the recommended serving size is 1 tablespoon. This is the same serving size that store bought creamers recommend.*

**Cinnamon Roll**

**CONTAINER SIZE:** 1 Quart (32 oz)                              **MY RATING:** ☆☆☆☆☆

## INGREDIENTS

- 14 oz. sweetened condensed milk
- 2 cups milk of choice
- 1 tbsp. ground cinnamon
  - OR 2 tsp. cinnamon extract
- 2 tbsp. brown sugar
- 1 tbsp. vanilla extract
  - OR 3 tbsp. vanilla syrup
- 1 tsp. cream cheese bakery emulsion

## DIRECTIONS

Combine sweetened condensed milk, cinnamon and brown sugar first. Mix well then mix in all other ingredients. Warm over medium heat for a few minutes until your mixture just starts to steam. Once it starts steaming, remove it from heat. Let it cool then transfer to your container.

*It is normal for ground spices to settle during storage. Just give it a quick shake before each use. If you prefer no settling spices, you can strain your mixture through a cheesecloth to filter out the spices as you put it in your container.*

## SUGAR FREE VERSION

- 3 cups milk of choice
- 1 cup sugar free cinnamon roll syrup

*Put in your container and shake. No need to heat.*

## DAIRY FREE VERSION

Follow instructions above but use these substitutions:
- 1 can sweetened condensed coconut milk OR sweetened condensed oat milk
- 2 1/4 cups milk alternative of choice (or more as needed)

## EXPIRATION DATE

Use the expiration date listed on the milk or milk substitute that you used.

## NOTES

*Cinnamon Roll Coffee Creamer*

*NUTRITIONAL FACTS: Homemade coffee creamer has less sugar, carbs, and calories than most store bought creamers. You can find nutritional fact calculators online to determine your exact nutritional facts based on the exact ingredients that you use. When comparing to store bought creamers, the recommended serving size is 1 tablespoon. This is the same serving size that store bought creamers recommend.*

**Cinnamon Vanilla**

**CONTAINER SIZE:** 1 Quart (32 oz)

**MY RATING:** ☆ ☆ ☆ ☆ ☆

## INGREDIENTS

- 14 oz. sweetened condensed milk
- 2 cups milk of choice
- 2 tsp. vanilla extract
    - OR 2 tbsp. vanilla syrup
- 1 tsp. ground cinnamon
    - OR 1 tsp. cinnamon extract

## DIRECTIONS

Combine sweetened condensed milk and cinnamon. Mix well then mix in all other ingredients. Warm over medium heat for a few minutes until your mixture just starts to steam. Once it starts steaming, remove it from heat. Let it cool then transfer to your container. *It is normal for ground spices to settle during storage. Just give it a quick shake before each use. If you prefer no settling spices, you can strain your mixture through a cheesecloth to filter out the spices as you put it in your container.*

## SUGAR FREE VERSION

- 3 cups milk of choice
- 1/2 cup sugar free cinnamon syrup
- 1/2 cup sugar free vanilla syrup

*Put in your container and shake. No need to heat.*

## DAIRY FREE VERSION

Follow instructions above but use these substitutions:
- 1 can sweetened condensed coconut milk OR sweetened condensed oat milk
- 2 1/4 cups milk alternative of choice (or more as needed)

## EXPIRATION DATE

Use the expiration date listed on the milk or milk substitute that you used.

## NOTES

*Cinnamon Vanilla Coffee Creamer*

*NUTRITIONAL FACTS: Homemade coffee creamer has less sugar, carbs, and calories than most store bought creamers. You can find nutritional fact calculators online to determine your exact nutritional facts based on the exact ingredients that you use. When comparing to store bought creamers, the recommended serving size is 1 tablespoon. This is the same serving size that store bought creamers recommend.*

# Coconut & Chocolate Bar

**CONTAINER SIZE:** 1 Quart (32 oz)

**MY RATING:** ☆☆☆☆☆

*"Popular Candy Bar Flavor"*

## INGREDIENTS

- 14 oz. sweetened condensed milk
- 2 cups milk of choice
- 2 tbsp. unsweetened cocoa powder
    - OR 4 tbsp. mocha syrup
- 2 tsp. coconut extract
    - OR 4 tbsp. coconut syrup
- 1 tsp. almond extract
    - OR 1 tsp. almond bakery emulsion

## DIRECTIONS

Combine sweetened condensed milk and cocoa powder first. Mix well then mix in all other ingredients. Warm over medium heat for a few minutes until your mixture just starts to steam. Once it starts steaming, remove it from heat. Let it cool then transfer to your container.

## SUGAR FREE VERSION

- 3 cups milk of choice
- 1/2 cup sugar free mocha syrup
- 1/4 cup sugar free coconut syrup
- 1/4 cup sugar free almond syrup

*Put in your container and shake. No need to heat.*

## DAIRY FREE VERSION

Follow instructions above but use these substitutions:
- 1 can sweetened condensed coconut milk OR sweetened condensed oat milk
- 2 1/4 cups milk alternative of choice (or more as needed)

## EXPIRATION DATE

Use the expiration date listed on the milk or milk substitute that you used.

## NOTES

*Coconut & Chocolate Bar Coffee Creamer*

*NUTRITIONAL FACTS: Homemade coffee creamer has less sugar, carbs, and calories than most store bought creamers. You can find nutritional fact calculators online to determine your exact nutritional facts based on the exact ingredients that you use. When comparing to store bought creamers, the recommended serving size is 1 tablespoon. This is the same serving size that store bought creamers recommend.*

Coconut & Créme

**CONTAINER SIZE:** 1 Quart (32 oz)

**MY RATING:** ☆ ☆ ☆ ☆ ☆

## INGREDIENTS

- 14 oz. sweetened condensed milk
- 2 cups coconut milk or milk of choice
- 1 tsp. vanilla extract
  - OR 1 tbsp. vanilla syrup
- 2 tsp. coconut extract
  - OR 2 tbsp. coconut syrup

## DIRECTIONS

Combine all ingredients, mix well. Warm over medium heat for a few minutes until your mixture just starts to steam. Once it starts steaming, remove it from heat. Let it cool then transfer to your container.

## SUGAR FREE VERSION

- 3 cups milk of choice
- 1 cup sugar free coconut syrup

*Put in your container and shake. No need to heat.*

## DAIRY FREE VERSION

Follow instructions above but use these substitutions:
- 1 can sweetened condensed coconut milk
- 2 1/4 cups of coconut milk

## EXPIRATION DATE

Use the expiration date listed on the milk or milk substitute that you used.

## NOTES

*Coconut & Creme Coffee Creamer*

*NUTRITIONAL FACTS: Homemade coffee creamer has less sugar, carbs, and calories than most store bought creamers. You can find nutritional fact calculators online to determine your exact nutritional facts based on the exact ingredients that you use. When comparing to store bought creamers, the recommended serving size is 1 tablespoon. This is the same serving size that store bought creamers recommend.*

# Coffee & Rum Liqueur

**CONTAINER SIZE:** 1 Quart (32 oz)

**MY RATING:** ☆☆☆☆☆

## INGREDIENTS

- 14 oz. sweetened condensed milk
- 2 cups milk of choice
- 1 tsp. espresso powder
- 1 tsp. vanilla extract
    - OR 1 tbsp. vanilla syrup
- 2-3 tsp. rum extract

## DIRECTIONS

Combine sweetened condensed milk and espresso powder first, mix well. Then add in all other ingredients. Warm over medium heat for a few minutes until your mixture just starts to steam. Once it starts steaming, remove it from heat. Let it cool then transfer to your container.

## SUGAR FREE VERSION

- 3 cups milk of choice
- 1 cup sugar free Coffee Liqueur syrup
    - OR 1 cup sugar free Espresso syrup
    - 1-2 tsp. rum extract

*Put in your container and shake. No need to heat.*

## DAIRY FREE VERSION

Follow instructions above but use these substitutions:
- 1 can sweetened condensed coconut milk OR sweetened condensed oat milk
- 2 1/4 cups milk alternative of choice (or more as needed)

## EXPIRATION DATE

Use the expiration date listed on the milk or milk substitute that you used.

## NOTES

*Coffee & Rum Liqueur Coffee Creamer*

*NUTRITIONAL FACTS: Homemade coffee creamer has less sugar, carbs, and calories than most store bought creamers. You can find nutritional fact calculators online to determine your exact nutritional facts based on the exact ingredients that you use. When comparing to store bought creamers, the recommended serving size is 1 tablespoon. This is the same serving size that store bought creamers recommend.*

# Coffee Cake

**CONTAINER SIZE: 1 Quart (32 oz)**                              **MY RATING:** ☆ ☆ ☆ ☆ ☆

## INGREDIENTS

- 14 oz. sweetened condensed milk
- 2 cups milk of choice
- 2 tsp. vanilla extract
    - OR 2 tbsp. vanilla syrup
- 2 tsp. cake batter extract
    - OR 2 tbsp. birthday cake syrup
- 1 tbsp. espresso powder
    - OR 2 tbsp. espresso syrup

## DIRECTIONS

Combine sweetened condensed milk and espresso powder first. Mix well then mix in all other ingredients. Warm over medium heat for a few minutes until your mixture just starts to steam. Once it starts steaming, remove it from heat. Let it cool then transfer to your container.

## SUGAR FREE VERSION

- 3 cups milk of choice
- 1/2 cup sugar free espresso syrup
- 1/2 cup sugar free birthday cake syrup

*Put in your container and shake. No need to heat.*

## DAIRY FREE VERSION

Follow instructions above but use these substitutions:
- 1 can sweetened condensed coconut milk OR sweetened condensed oat milk
- 2 1/4 cups milk alternative of choice (or more as needed)

## EXPIRATION DATE

Use the expiration date listed on the milk or milk substitute that you used.

## NOTES

Coffee Cake Coffee Creamer

*NUTRITIONAL FACTS: Homemade coffee creamer has less sugar, carbs, and calories than most store bought creamers. You can find nutritional fact calculators online to determine your exact nutritional facts based on the exact ingredients that you use. When comparing to store bought creamers, the recommended serving size is 1 tablespoon. This is the same serving size that store bought creamers recommend.*

**CONTAINER SIZE:** 1 Quart (32 oz)                        **MY RATING:** ☆☆☆☆☆

## INGREDIENTS

- 14 oz. sweetened condensed milk
- 2 cups milk of choice
- 1 + 1/2 tbsp. cookie butter emulsion
    - OR 5 tbsp. cookie butter/speculoos syrup
    - OR 1/4 cup real cookie butter

## DIRECTIONS

Combine all ingredients and mix well. Warm over medium heat for a few minutes until your mixture just starts to steam. Once it starts steaming, remove it from heat. Let it cool then transfer to your container.

## SUGAR FREE VERSION

- 3 cups milk of choice
- 1 cup sugar free cookie butter / speculoos syrup

*Put in your container and shake. No need to heat.*

## DAIRY FREE VERSION

Follow instructions above but use these substitutions:
- 1 can sweetened condensed coconut milk OR sweetened condensed oat milk
- 2 1/4 cups milk alternative of choice (or more as needed)

## EXPIRATION DATE

Use the expiration date listed on the milk or milk substitute that you used.

## NOTES

*Cookie Butter Coffee Creamer*

*NUTRITIONAL FACTS: Homemade coffee creamer has less sugar, carbs, and calories than most store bought creamers. You can find nutritional fact calculators online to determine your exact nutritional facts based on the exact ingredients that you use. When comparing to store bought creamers, the recommended serving size is 1 tablespoon. This is the same serving size that store bought creamers recommend.*

**CONTAINER SIZE:** 1 Quart (32 oz)

**MY RATING:** ☆☆☆☆☆

## INGREDIENTS

- 14 oz. sweetened condensed milk
- 2 cups milk of choice
- 2 tbsp. unsweetened cocoa powder
  - OR 4 tbsp. mocha syrup
- 2 tbsp. brown sugar
- 2 tsp. vanilla extract
  - OR 2 tbsp. vanilla syrup

## DIRECTIONS

Combine sweetened condensed milk and cocoa powder first. Mix well then mix in all other ingredients. Warm over medium heat for a few minutes until your mixture just starts to steam. Once it starts steaming, remove it from heat. Let it cool then transfer to your container.

*It is normal for ground spices to settle during storage. Just give it a quick shake before each use. If you prefer no settling spices, you can strain your mixture through a cheesecloth to filter out the spices as you put it in your container.*

## SUGAR FREE VERSION

- 3 cups milk of choice
- 1 cup sugar free cookie dough syrup

*Put in your container and shake. No need to heat.*

## DAIRY FREE VERSION

Follow instructions above but use these substitutions:
- 1 can sweetened condensed coconut milk OR sweetened condensed oat milk
- 2 1/4 cups milk alternative of choice (or more as needed)

## EXPIRATION DATE

Use the expiration date listed on the milk or milk substitute that you used.

## NOTES

*Cookie Dough Coffee Creamer*

*NUTRITIONAL FACTS: Homemade coffee creamer has less sugar, carbs, and calories than most store bought creamers. You can find nutritional fact calculators online to determine your exact nutritional facts based on the exact ingredients that you use. When comparing to store bought creamers, the recommended serving size is 1 tablespoon. This is the same serving size that store bought creamers recommend.*

# Cookies & Cream

**CONTAINER SIZE:** 1 Quart (32 oz)

**MY RATING:** ☆☆☆☆☆

## INGREDIENTS

- 14 oz. sweetened condensed milk
- 2 cups milk of choice
- 1 tbsp. black dutched cocoa powder
  - OR 1-2 tbsp. special dark cocoa powder
- 2 tsp. vanilla extract
  - OR 1 tbsp. vanilla syrup
- 1 tbsp. powdered sugar

## DIRECTIONS

Combine cocoa powder and sweetened condensed milk first, mix well. Then add in all other ingredients. Warm over medium heat for a few minutes until your mixture just starts to steam. Once it starts steaming, remove it from heat. Let it cool then transfer to your container.

## SUGAR FREE VERSION

- 3 cups milk of choice
- 1 cup sugar free cookies & cream syrup

*Put in your container and shake. No need to heat.*

## DAIRY FREE VERSION

Follow instructions above but use these substitutions:
- 1 can sweetened condensed coconut milk OR sweetened condensed oat milk
- 2 1/4 cups milk alternative of choice (or more as needed)

## EXPIRATION DATE

Use the expiration date listed on the milk or milk substitute that you used.

## NOTES

*Cookies & Cream Coffee Creamer*

*NUTRITIONAL FACTS: Homemade coffee creamer has less sugar, carbs, and calories than most store bought creamers. You can find nutritional fact calculators online to determine your exact nutritional facts based on the exact ingredients that you use. When comparing to store bought creamers, the recommended serving size is 1 tablespoon. This is the same serving size that store bought creamers recommend.*

## Crème Brûlée

**CONTAINER SIZE:** 1 Quart (32 oz)

**MY RATING:** ☆☆☆☆☆

## INGREDIENTS

- 14 oz. sweetened condensed milk
- 2 cups milk of choice
- 2 tsp. vanilla extract
  - OR 2 tbsp. vanilla syrup
- 1/4 cup brown sugar

## DIRECTIONS

Combine all ingredients and mix well. Warm over medium heat for a few minutes until your mixture just starts to steam. Once it starts steaming, remove it from heat. Let it cool then transfer to your container.

## SUGAR FREE VERSION

- 3 cups milk of choice
- 3/4 cup sugar free brown sugar syrup
- 1/4 cup sugar free vanilla syrup

*Put in your container and shake. No need to heat.*

## DAIRY FREE VERSION

Follow instructions above but use these substitutions:
- 1 can sweetened condensed coconut milk OR sweetened condensed oat milk
- 2 1/4 cups milk alternative of choice (or more as needed)

## EXPIRATION DATE

Use the expiration date listed on the milk or milk substitute that you used.

## NOTES

*Crème Brûlée Coffee Creamer*

*NUTRITIONAL FACTS: Homemade coffee creamer has less sugar, carbs, and calories than most store bought creamers. You can find nutritional fact calculators online to determine your exact nutritional facts based on the exact ingredients that you use. When comparing to store bought creamers, the recommended serving size is 1 tablespoon. This is the same serving size that store bought creamers recommend.*

# Eggnog Creamer

**CONTAINER SIZE:** 1 Quart (32 oz)

**MY RATING:** ☆☆☆☆☆

## INGREDIENTS

- 14 oz. sweetened condensed milk
- 2 cups milk of choice
- 1 tsp. vanilla extract
    - OR 1 tbsp. vanilla syrup
- 1 tsp. ground nutmeg
- 1/2 tsp. ground cinnamon
    - OR 1/2 tsp. cinnamon extract
- 1 tsp. rum extract *(optional)*

## DIRECTIONS

Combine sweetened condensed milk and powders first. Mix well then mix in all other ingredients. Warm over medium heat for a few minutes until your mixture just starts to steam. Once it starts steaming, remove it from heat. Let it cool then transfer to your container.

*It is normal for ground spices to settle during storage. Just give it a quick shake before each use. If you prefer no settling spices, you can strain your mixture through a cheesecloth to filter out the spices as you put it in your container.*

## SUGAR FREE VERSION

- 3 cups milk of choice
- 1 cup sugar free Eggnog syrup

*Put in your container and shake. No need to heat.*

## DAIRY FREE VERSION

Follow instructions above but use these substitutions:

- 1 can sweetened condensed coconut milk OR sweetened condensed oat milk
- 2 1/4 cups milk alternative of choice (or more as needed)

## EXPIRATION DATE

Use the expiration date listed on the milk or milk substitute that you used.

## NOTES

Eggnog Coffee Creamer

*NUTRITIONAL FACTS: Homemade coffee creamer has less sugar, carbs, and calories than most store bought creamers. You can find nutritional fact calculators online to determine your exact nutritional facts based on the exact ingredients that you use. When comparing to store bought creamers, the recommended serving size is 1 tablespoon. This is the same serving size that store bought creamers recommend.*

**CONTAINER SIZE:** 1 Quart (32 oz)

**MY RATING:** ☆ ☆ ☆ ☆ ☆

## INGREDIENTS

- 14 oz. sweetened condensed milk
- 2 cups milk of choice
- 1-2 tsp. espresso powder
    - OR 1-2 tbsp. espresso syrup
- 1 tsp. vanilla extract
    - OR 1 tbsp. vanilla syrup

## DIRECTIONS

Combine sweetened condensed milk and espresso powder first. Mix well then mix in all other ingredients. Warm over medium heat for a few minutes until your mixture just starts to steam. Once it starts steaming, remove it from heat. Let it cool then transfer to your container.

## SUGAR FREE VERSION

- 3 cups milk of choice
- 1 cup sugar free espresso syrup

*Put in your container and shake. No need to heat.*

## DAIRY FREE VERSION

Follow instructions above but use these substitutions:
- 1 can sweetened condensed coconut milk OR sweetened condensed oat milk
- 2 1/4 cups milk alternative of choice (or more as needed)

## EXPIRATION DATE

Use the expiration date listed on the milk or milk substitute that you used.

## NOTES

*Espresso Coffee Creamer*

*NUTRITIONAL FACTS: Homemade coffee creamer has less sugar, carbs, and calories than most store bought creamers. You can find nutritional fact calculators online to determine your exact nutritional facts based on the exact ingredients that you use. When comparing to store bought creamers, the recommended serving size is 1 tablespoon. This is the same serving size that store bought creamers recommend.*

**CONTAINER SIZE: 1 Quart (32 oz)**

**MY RATING:** ☆☆☆☆☆

## INGREDIENTS

- 14 oz. sweetened condensed milk
- 2 cups milk of choice
- 1 tbsp. vanilla extract
    - OR 4 tbsp. vanilla syrup
- 1 tsp. hazelnut extract or emulsion
    - OR 1 tbsp. hazelnut syrup

## DIRECTIONS

Combine all ingredients and mix well. Warm over medium heat for a few minutes until your mixture just starts to steam. Once it starts steaming, remove it from heat. Let it cool then transfer to your container.

## SUGAR FREE VERSION

- 3 cups milk of choice
- 1 cup sugar free French vanilla syrup

*Put in your container and shake. No need to heat.*

## DAIRY FREE VERSION

Follow instructions above but use these substitutions:
- 1 can sweetened condensed coconut milk OR sweetened condensed oat milk
- 2 1/4 cups milk alternative of choice (or more as needed)

## EXPIRATION DATE

Use the expiration date listed on the milk or milk substitute that you used.

## NOTES

*French Vanilla Coffee Creamer*

*NUTRITIONAL FACTS: Homemade coffee creamer has less sugar, carbs, and calories than most store bought creamers. You can find nutritional fact calculators online to determine your exact nutritional facts based on the exact ingredients that you use. When comparing to store bought creamers, the recommended serving size is 1 tablespoon. This is the same serving size that store bought creamers recommend.*

# Frosted Gingerbread

**CONTAINER SIZE:** 1 Quart (32 oz)

**MY RATING:** ☆☆☆☆☆

## INGREDIENTS

- 14 oz. sweetened condensed milk
- 1 tbsp. brown sugar
- 1 tbsp. molasses
- 1 tsp. ground ginger
- 1/2 tsp. ground allspice
- 1/2 tsp. ground cinnamon
- 2 cups milk of choice
- 1 tsp. vanilla extract
    - OR 1 tbsp. vanilla syrup

## DIRECTIONS

Combine sweetened condensed milk and all dried spice ingredients, brown sugar, and molasses mix well. Then add in milk and extract. Warm over medium heat for a few minutes until your mixture just starts to steam. Once it starts steaming, remove it from heat. Let it cool then transfer to your container.

*It is normal for ground spices to settle during storage. Just give it a quick shake before each use. If you prefer no settling spices, you can strain your mixture through a cheesecloth to filter out the spices as you put it in your container.*

## SUGAR FREE VERSION

- 3 cups milk of choice
- 1 cup sugar free gingerbread cookie syrup

*Put in your container and shake. No need to heat.*

## DAIRY FREE VERSION

Follow instructions above but use these substitutions:
- 1 can sweetened condensed coconut milk OR sweetened condensed oat milk
- 2 1/4 cups milk alternative of choice (or more as needed)

## EXPIRATION DATE

Use the expiration date listed on the milk or milk substitute that you used.

## NOTES

*Frosted Gingerbread Coffee Creamer*

*NUTRITIONAL FACTS: Homemade coffee creamer has less sugar, carbs, and calories than most store bought creamers. You can find nutritional fact calculators online to determine your exact nutritional facts based on the exact ingredients that you use. When comparing to store bought creamers, the recommended serving size is 1 tablespoon. This is the same serving size that store bought creamers recommend.*

**Fun Confetti**

**CONTAINER SIZE:** 1 Quart (32 oz)

**MY RATING:** ☆☆☆☆☆

## INGREDIENTS

- 14 oz. sweetened condensed milk
- 2 cups milk of choice
- 2 tsp. vanilla extract
  - OR 2 tbsp. vanilla syrup
- 1 tsp. butter extract
  - OR 1 tbsp. butter
- 1/2 tbsp. brown sugar
- OPTIONAL: 1-2 tbsp. sprinkles for pretty confetti

## DIRECTIONS

Combine all ingredients (except sprinkles), mix well. Warm over medium heat for a few minutes until your mixture just starts to steam. Once it starts steaming, remove it from heat. Let it cool then transfer to your container. Then add in optional sprinkles.

## SUGAR FREE VERSION

- 3 cups milk of choice
- 1 cup sugar free cake batter syrup
- 1-2 tbsp. sugar free sprinkles

*Put in your container and shake. No need to heat.*

## DAIRY FREE VERSION

Follow instructions above but use these substitutions:

- 1 can sweetened condensed coconut milk OR sweetened condensed oat milk
- 2 1/4 cups milk alternative of choice (or more as needed)

## EXPIRATION DATE

Use the expiration date listed on the milk or milk substitute that you used.

## NOTES

*Fun Confetti Cake Coffee Creamer*

*NUTRITIONAL FACTS: Homemade coffee creamer has less sugar, carbs, and calories than most store bought creamers. You can find nutritional fact calculators online to determine your exact nutritional facts based on the exact ingredients that you use. When comparing to store bought creamers, the recommended serving size is 1 tablespoon. This is the same serving size that store bought creamers recommend.*

## Hazelnut Mocha

**CONTAINER SIZE:** 1 Quart (32 oz)

**MY RATING:** ☆☆☆☆☆

## INGREDIENTS

- 14 oz. sweetened condensed milk
- 2 cups milk of choice
- 2 tbsp. unsweetened cocoa powder
- 1 tsp. vanilla extract
    - OR 1 tbsp. vanilla syrup
- 2-3 tsp. hazelnut extract or emulsion
    - OR 2-3 tbsp. hazelnut syrup

## DIRECTIONS

Combine sweetened condensed milk and cocoa powder first. Mix well then add in all other ingredients. Warm over medium heat for a few minutes until your mixture just starts to steam. Once it starts steaming, remove it from heat. Let it cool then transfer to your container.

*It is normal for ground spices to settle during storage. Just give it a quick shake before each use. If you prefer no set-tling spices, you can strain your mixture through a cheesecloth to filter out the spices as you put it in your container.*

## SUGAR FREE VERSION

- 3 cups milk of choice
- 2/3 cup sugar free hazelnut syrup
- 1/3 cup sugar free mocha syrup

*Put in your container and shake. No need to heat.*

## DAIRY FREE VERSION

Follow instructions above but use these substitutions:
- 1 can sweetened condensed coconut milk OR sweetened condensed oat milk
- 2 1/4 cups milk alternative of choice (or more as needed)

## EXPIRATION DATE

Use the expiration date listed on the milk or milk substitute that you used.

## NOTES

*Hazelnut Mocha Coffee Creamer*

*NUTRITIONAL FACTS: Homemade coffee creamer has less sugar, carbs, and calories than most store bought creamers. You can find nutritional fact calculators online to determine your exact nutritional facts based on the exact ingredients that you use. When comparing to store bought creamers, the recommended serving size is 1 tablespoon. This is the same serving size that store bought creamers recommend.*

# Hazelnut

**CONTAINER SIZE:** 1 Quart (32 oz)

**MY RATING:** ☆ ☆ ☆ ☆ ☆

## INGREDIENTS

- 14 oz. sweetened condensed milk
- 2 cups milk of choice
- 1 tsp. vanilla extract
    - OR 1 tbsp. vanilla syrup
- 1-2 tsp. hazelnut extract or emulsion
    - OR 2 tbsp. hazelnut syrup

## DIRECTIONS

Combine all ingredients, mix well. Warm over medium heat for a few minutes until your mixture just starts to steam. Once it starts steaming, remove it from heat. Let it cool then transfer to your container.

## SUGAR FREE VERSION

- 3 cups milk of choice
- 1 cup sugar free hazelnut syrup

*Put in your container and shake. No need to heat.*

## DAIRY FREE VERSION

Follow instructions above but use these substitutions:
- 1 can sweetened condensed coconut milk OR sweetened condensed oat milk
- 2 1/4 cups milk alternative of choice (or more as needed)

## EXPIRATION DATE

Use the expiration date listed on the milk or milk substitute that you used.

## NOTES

*Hazelnut Coffee Creamer*

*NUTRITIONAL FACTS: Homemade coffee creamer has less sugar, carbs, and calories than most store bought creamers. You can find nutritional fact calculators online to determine your exact nutritional facts based on the exact ingredients that you use. When comparing to store bought creamers, the recommended serving size is 1 tablespoon. This is the same serving size that store bought creamers recommend.*

# Horchata

**CONTAINER SIZE:** 1 Quart (32 oz)

**MY RATING:** ☆☆☆☆☆

## INGREDIENTS

- 14 oz. sweetened condensed milk
- 2 cups rice milk
- 1 tsp. vanilla extract
    - OR 1 tbsp. vanilla syrup
- 1 tsp. ground cinnamon
    - OR 2 tsp. cinnamon extract
- 1 tbsp. brown sugar

(Make your own rice milk by blending together 1/2 cup cooked white rice with 2 cups of milk. Strain.)

## DIRECTIONS

Combine sweetened condensed milk, cinnamon and brown sugar first. Mix well then mix in all other ingredients. Warm over medium heat for a few minutes until your mixture just starts to steam. Once it starts steaming, remove it from heat. Let it cool then transfer to your container.

*It is normal for ground spices to settle during storage. Just give it a quick shake before each use. If you prefer no settling spices, you can strain your mixture through a cheesecloth to filter out the spices as you put it in your container.*

## SUGAR FREE VERSION

- 3 cups milk of choice
- 1 cup sugar free horchata syrup

*Put in your container and shake. No need to heat.*

## DAIRY FREE VERSION

Follow instructions above but use these substitutions:
- 1 can sweetened condensed coconut milk OR sweetened condensed oat milk

## EXPIRATION DATE

Use the expiration date listed on the milk or milk substitute that you used.

## NOTES

*Horchata Coffee Creamer*

*NUTRITIONAL FACTS: Homemade coffee creamer has less sugar, carbs, and calories than most store bought creamers. You can find nutritional fact calculators online to determine your exact nutritional facts based on the exact ingredients that you use. When comparing to store bought creamers, the recommended serving size is 1 tablespoon. This is the same serving size that store bought creamers recommend.*

**CONTAINER SIZE:** 1 Quart (32 oz)                    **MY RATING:** ☆☆☆☆☆

## INGREDIENTS

- 14 oz. sweetened condensed milk
- 2 cups milk of choice
- 1 tsp. vanilla extract
    - OR 1 tbsp. vanilla syrup
- 1 tbsp. marshmallow fluff
    - OR 2 tbsp. marshmallow syrup
- 1/4 cup unsweetened cocoa powder

## DIRECTIONS

Combine sweetened condensed milk, marshmallow fluff and cocoa powder first. Mix well then mix in all other ingredients. Warm over medium heat for a few minutes until your mixture just starts to steam. Once it starts steaming, remove it from heat. Let it cool then transfer to your container.

*It is normal for ground spices to settle during storage. Just give it a quick shake before each use. If you prefer no settling spices, you can strain your mixture through a cheesecloth to filter out the spices as you put it in your container.*

## SUGAR FREE VERSION

- 3 cups milk of choice
- 3/4 cup sugar free mocha syrup
- 1/4 cup sugar free marshmallow syrup

*Put in your container and shake. No need to heat.*

## DAIRY FREE VERSION

Follow instructions above but use these substitutions:

- 1 can sweetened condensed coconut milk OR sweetened condensed oat milk
- 2 1/4 cups milk alternative of choice (or more as needed)

## EXPIRATION DATE

Use the expiration date listed on the milk or milk substitute that you used.

## NOTES

*NUTRITIONAL FACTS: Homemade coffee creamer has less sugar, carbs, and calories than most store bought creamers. You can find nutritional fact calculators online to determine your exact nutritional facts based on the exact ingredients that you use. When comparing to store bought creamers, the recommended serving size is 1 tablespoon. This is the same serving size that store bought creamers recommend.*

**Irish Cream**

**CONTAINER SIZE:** 1 Quart (32 oz)

**MY RATING:** ☆☆☆☆☆

## INGREDIENTS

- 14 oz. sweetened condensed milk
- 2 cups milk of choice
- 2 tbsp. unsweetened cocoa powder
  - OR 4 tbsp. mocha syrup
- 1 tsp. espresso powder
- 1 tsp. vanilla extract
  - OR 1 tbsp. vanilla syrup
- 1/2 tsp. almond extract
  - OR 1/2 tsp. almond bakery emulsion

## DIRECTIONS

Combine sweetened condensed milk and powders first. Mix well then mix in all other ingredients. Warm over medium heat for a few minutes until your mixture just starts to steam. Once it starts steaming, remove it from heat. Let it cool then transfer to your container.

*It is normal for ground spices to settle during storage. Just give it a quick shake before each use. If you prefer no settling spices, you can strain your mixture through a cheesecloth to filter out the spices as you put it in your container.*

## SUGAR FREE VERSION

- 3 cups milk of choice
- 1 cup sugar free Irish cream syrup

*Put in your container and shake. No need to heat.*

## DAIRY FREE VERSION

Follow instructions above but use these substitutions:
- 1 can sweetened condensed coconut milk OR sweetened condensed oat milk
- 2 1/4 cups milk alternative of choice (or more as needed)

## EXPIRATION DATE

Use the expiration date listed on the milk or milk substitute that you used.

## NOTES

*Irish Cream Coffee Creamer*

*NUTRITIONAL FACTS: Homemade coffee creamer has less sugar, carbs, and calories than most store bought creamers. You can find nutritional fact calculators online to determine your exact nutritional facts based on the exact ingredients that you use. When comparing to store bought creamers, the recommended serving size is 1 tablespoon. This is the same serving size that store bought creamers recommend.*

# Italian Sweet Cream

**CONTAINER SIZE:** 1 Quart (32 oz)

**MY RATING:** ☆☆☆☆☆

## INGREDIENTS

- 14 oz. sweetened condensed milk
- 2 cups milk of choice
- 1-2 tsp. vanilla extract
  - OR 1-2 tbsp. vanilla syrup
- 1-2 tsp. almond extract
  - OR 1-2 tbsp. almond syrup

## DIRECTIONS

Combine all ingredients. Mix well. Warm over medium heat for a few minutes until your mixture just starts to steam. Once it starts steaming, remove it from heat. Let it cool then transfer to your container.

## SUGAR FREE VERSION

- 3 cups milk of choice
- 1/2 cup sugar free vanilla syrup
- 1/2 cup sugar free syrup

*Put in your container and shake. No need to heat.*

## DAIRY FREE VERSION

Follow instructions above but use these substitutions:
- 1 can sweetened condensed coconut milk OR sweetened condensed oat milk
- 2 1/4 cups milk alternative of choice (or more as needed)

## EXPIRATION DATE

Use the expiration date listed on the milk or milk substitute that you used.

## NOTES

*Italian Sweet Cream Coffee Creamer*

*NUTRITIONAL FACTS: Homemade coffee creamer has less sugar, carbs, and calories than most store bought creamers. You can find nutritional fact calculators online to determine your exact nutritional facts based on the exact ingredients that you use. When comparing to store bought creamers, the recommended serving size is 1 tablespoon. This is the same serving size that store bought creamers recommend.*

**CONTAINER SIZE:** 1 Quart (32 oz)    MY RATING: ☆ ☆ ☆ ☆ ☆

## INGREDIENTS

- 14 oz. sweetened condensed milk
- 2 cups milk of choice
- 2 tbsp. brown sugar
- 2 tbsp. pure maple syrup
  - OR pancake syrup
  - OR 1 tsp. maple extract
- 1 tsp. vanilla extract
  - OR 1 tbsp. vanilla syrup

## DIRECTIONS

Combine all ingredients. Mix well. Warm over medium heat for a few minutes until your mixture just starts to steam. Once it starts steaming, remove it from heat. Let it cool then transfer to your container.

## SUGAR FREE VERSION

- 3 cups milk of choice
- 1/2 cup sugar free maple syrup
- 1/2 cup sugar free brown sugar syrup

*Put in your container and shake. No need to heat.*

## DAIRY FREE VERSION

Follow instructions above but use these substitutions:

- 1 can sweetened condensed coconut milk OR sweetened condensed oat milk
- 2 1/4 cups milk alternative of choice (or more as needed)

## EXPIRATION DATE

Use the expiration date listed on the milk or milk substitute that you used.

## NOTES

*Maple & Brown Sugar Coffee Creamer*

*NUTRITIONAL FACTS: Homemade coffee creamer has less sugar, carbs, and calories than most store bought creamers. You can find nutritional fact calculators online to determine your exact nutritional facts based on the exact ingredients that you use. When comparing to store bought creamers, the recommended serving size is 1 tablespoon. This is the same serving size that store bought creamers recommend.*

# Marshmallow & Rice Treat

**CONTAINER SIZE:** 1 Quart (32 oz)

**MY RATING:** ☆☆☆☆☆

## INGREDIENTS

- 14 oz. sweetened condensed milk
- 2 cups rice milk
- 1 tsp. vanilla extract
  - OR 1 tbsp. vanilla syrup
- 1 tsp. butter extract
  - OR 1 tbsp. butter
- 2 tbsp. marshmallow fluff

## DIRECTIONS

Combine all ingredients, mix well. Warm over medium heat for a few minutes until your mixture just starts to steam. Once it starts steaming, remove it from heat. Let it cool then transfer to your container.

## SUGAR FREE VERSION

- 3 cups rice milk
- 1 cup sugar free marshmallow syrup

*Put in your container and shake. No need to heat.*

## DAIRY FREE VERSION

Follow instructions above but use these substitutions:
- 1 can sweetened condensed coconut milk OR sweetened condensed oat milk

## EXPIRATION DATE

Use the expiration date listed on the milk or milk substitute that you used.

## NOTES

*Marshmallow & Rice Treat Coffee Creamer*

*NUTRITIONAL FACTS: Homemade coffee creamer has less sugar, carbs, and calories than most store bought creamers. You can find nutritional fact calculators online to determine your exact nutritional facts based on the exact ingredients that you use. When comparing to store bought creamers, the recommended serving size is 1 tablespoon. This is the same serving size that store bought creamers recommend.*

# Mexican Hot Chocolate

**CONTAINER SIZE:** 1 Quart (32 oz)

**MY RATING:** ☆☆☆☆☆

## INGREDIENTS

- 14 oz. sweetened condensed milk
- 2 cups milk of choice
- 1/4 cup unsweetened cocoa powder
- 1 tsp. vanilla extract
  - OR 1 tbsp. vanilla syrup
- 1 tsp. ground cinnamon
  - OR 1 tsp. cinnamon extract
- 1 tsp. chili powder
- Pinch of cayenne pepper for an extra kick

## DIRECTIONS

Combine sweetened condensed milk, cocoa powder, cinnamon and chili powder, mix well. Then add in all other ingredients, mix well. Warm over medium heat for a few minutes until your mixture just starts to steam. Once it starts steaming, remove it from heat. Let it cool then transfer to your container.

*It is normal for ground spices to settle during storage. Just give it a quick shake before each use. If you prefer no settling spices, you can strain your mixture through a cheesecloth to filter out the spices as you put it in your container.*

## SUGAR FREE VERSION

Follow all instructions above but make your own sweetened condensed milk using a sugar alternative like monk fruit, stevia, etc. Check out page 70! There are also several recipes available online depending on which sugar alternative you prefer.

## DAIRY FREE VERSION

Follow instructions above but use these substitutions:
- 1 can sweetened condensed coconut milk OR sweetened condensed oat milk
- 2 1/4 cups milk alternative of choice (or more as needed)

## EXPIRATION DATE

Use the expiration date listed on the milk or milk substitute that you used.

## NOTES

*Mexican Hot Chocolate Coffee Creamer*

*NUTRITIONAL FACTS: Homemade coffee creamer has less sugar, carbs, and calories than most store bought creamers. You can find nutritional fact calculators online to determine your exact nutritional facts based on the exact ingredients that you use. When comparing to store bought creamers, the recommended serving size is 1 tablespoon. This is the same serving size that store bought creamers recommend.*

**CONTAINER SIZE:** 1 Quart (32 oz)

**MY RATING:** ☆ ☆ ☆ ☆ ☆

*"Peppermint Mocha"*

## INGREDIENTS

- 14 oz. sweetened condensed milk
- 2 cups milk of choice
- 1/3 cup unsweetened cocoa powder
- 1 tsp. vanilla extract
    - OR 1 tbsp. vanilla syrup
- 1-2 tsp peppermint extract
    - OR 3 tbsp. peppermint syrup

## DIRECTIONS

Combine sweetened condensed milk and cocoa powder first. Mix well then mix in all other ingredients. Warm over medium heat for a few minutes until your mixture just starts to steam. Once it starts steaming, remove it from heat. Let it cool then transfer to your container.

*It is normal for ground spices to settle during storage. Just give it a quick shake before each use. If you prefer no settling spices, you can strain your mixture through a cheesecloth to filter out the spices as you put it in your container.*

## SUGAR FREE VERSION

- 3 cups milk of choice
- 1 cup sugar free mint chocolate syrup

*Put in your container and shake. No need to heat.*

## DAIRY FREE VERSION

Follow instructions above but use these substitutions:
- 1 can sweetened condensed coconut milk OR sweetened condensed oat milk
- 2 1/4 cups milk alternative of choice (or more as needed)

## EXPIRATION DATE

Use the expiration date listed on the milk or milk substitute that you used.

## NOTES

*Mint Chocolate Coffee Creamer*

*NUTRITIONAL FACTS: Homemade coffee creamer has less sugar, carbs, and calories than most store bought creamers. You can find nutritional fact calculators online to determine your exact nutritional facts based on the exact ingredients that you use. When comparing to store bought creamers, the recommended serving size is 1 tablespoon. This is the same serving size that store bought creamers recommend.*

# Nutty Caramel Chocolate Bar

**CONTAINER SIZE:**
1 Quart (32 oz)

*"Popular Candy Bar Flavor"*

**MY RATING:** ☆☆☆☆☆

## INGREDIENTS

- 14 oz. sweetened condensed milk
- 2 cups milk of choice
- 1/4 cup unsweetened cocoa powder
    - OR 1/2 cup mocha syrup
- 1 tsp. vanilla extract
    - OR 1 tbsp. vanilla syrup
- 2 tbsp. smooth peanut butter
- 3 tbsp. caramel sauce or syrup

## DIRECTIONS

Combine sweetened condensed milk and cocoa powder first. Mix well then mix in all other ingredients. Warm over medium heat for a few minutes until your mixture just starts to steam. Once it starts steaming, remove it from heat. Let it cool then transfer to your container.

*It is normal for ground spices to settle during storage. Just give it a quick shake before each use. If you prefer no settling spices, you can strain your mixture through a cheesecloth to filter out the spices as you put it in your container.*

## SUGAR FREE VERSION

- 3 cups milk of choice
- 1/2 cup sugar free mocha syrup
- 1/3 cup sugar free caramel syrup
- 2 tbsp. sugar free peanut butter cup syrup

*Put in your container and shake. No need to heat.*

## DAIRY FREE VERSION

Follow instructions above but use these substitutions:
- 1 can sweetened condensed coconut milk OR sweetened condensed oat milk
- 2 1/4 cups milk alternative of choice (or more as needed)

## EXPIRATION DATE

Use the expiration date listed on the milk or milk substitute that you used.

## NOTES

*Nutty Caramel Chocolate Bar Coffee Creamer*

*NUTRITIONAL FACTS: Homemade coffee creamer has less sugar, carbs, and calories than most store bought creamers. You can find nutritional fact calculators online to determine your exact nutritional facts based on the exact ingredients that you use. When comparing to store bought creamers, the recommended serving size is 1 tablespoon. This is the same serving size that store bought creamers recommend.*

# Orange Creamsicle

**CONTAINER SIZE:** 1 Quart (32 oz)                                                **MY RATING:** ☆☆☆☆☆

*"a.k.a. Fruity Cereal"*

## INGREDIENTS

- 14 oz. sweetened condensed milk
- 2 cups milk of choice
- 1 tsp. orange bakery emulsion
  - OR 1 tsp. orange extract
- 1 tsp. vanilla extract
  - OR 1 tbsp. vanilla syrup

## DIRECTIONS

Combine all ingredients, mix well. Warm over medium heat for a few minutes until your mixture just starts to steam. Once it starts steaming, remove it from heat. Let it cool then transfer to your container.

## SUGAR FREE VERSION

- 3 cups milk of choice
- 3/4 cup sugar free orange syrup
- 1/4 cup sugar free vanilla syrup

*Put in your container and shake. No need to heat.*

## DAIRY FREE VERSION

Follow instructions above but use these substitutions:

- 1 can sweetened condensed coconut milk OR sweetened condensed oat milk
- 2 1/4 cups milk alternative of choice (or more as needed)

## EXPIRATION DATE

Use the expiration date listed on the milk or milk substitute that you used.

## NOTES

*Orange Creamsicle Coffee Creamer*

*NUTRITIONAL FACTS: Homemade coffee creamer has less sugar, carbs, and calories than most store bought creamers. You can find nutritional fact calculators online to determine your exact nutritional facts based on the exact ingredients that you use. When comparing to store bought creamers, the recommended serving size is 1 tablespoon. This is the same serving size that store bought creamers recommend.*

**CONTAINER SIZE:** 1 Quart (32 oz)

MY RATING: ☆☆☆☆☆

*"Chocolate Covered Orange"*

## INGREDIENTS

- 14 oz. sweetened condensed milk
- 2 cups milk of choice
- 3 tbsp. unsweetened cocoa powder
- 2 tsp. orange bakery emulsion
  - OR 2 tsp. orange extract
- 1 tsp. vanilla extract
  - OR 1 tbsp. vanilla syrup

## DIRECTIONS

Combine sweetened condensed and cocoa powder first. Mix well then mix in all other ingredients. Warm over medium heat for a few minutes until your mixture just starts to steam. Once it starts steaming, remove it from heat. Let it cool then transfer to your container.

*It is normal for ground spices to settle during storage. Just give it a quick shake before each use. If you prefer no settling spices, you can strain your mixture through a cheesecloth to filter out the spices as you put it in your container.*

## SUGAR FREE VERSION

- 3 cups milk of choice
- 1/2 cup sugar free mocha syrup
- 1/4 cup sugar free vanilla syrup
- 1/4 cup sugar free orange syrup

*Put in your container and shake. No need to heat.*

## DAIRY FREE VERSION

Follow instructions above but use these substitutions:
- 1 can sweetened condensed coconut milk OR sweetened condensed oat milk
- 2 1/4 cups milk alternative of choice (or more as needed)

## EXPIRATION DATE

Use the expiration date listed on the milk or milk substitute that you used.

## NOTES

*Orange Micha Coffee Creamer*

*NUTRITIONAL FACTS: Homemade coffee creamer has less sugar, carbs, and calories than most store bought creamers. You can find nutritional fact calculators online to determine your exact nutritional facts based on the exact ingredients that you use. When comparing to store bought creamers, the recommended serving size is 1 tablespoon. This is the same serving size that store bought creamers recommend.*

# Peanut Butter Cup

**CONTAINER SIZE:** 1 Quart (32 oz)

**MY RATING:** ☆☆☆☆☆

*"Popular Candy Bar Flavor"*

## INGREDIENTS

- 14 oz. sweetened condensed milk
- 2 cups milk of choice
- 2 tbsp. smooth peanut butter
- 2 tbsp. unsweetened cocoa powder
- 1 tbsp. vanilla extract
  - OR 3 tbsp. vanilla syrup

## DIRECTIONS

Combine sweetened condensed milk, peanut butter, and cocoa powder first. Mix well then mix in all other ingredients. Warm over medium heat for a few minutes until your mixture just starts to steam. Once it starts steaming, remove it from heat. Let it cool then transfer to your container.

## SUGAR FREE VERSION

- 3 cups milk of choice
- 1 cup sugar free peanut butter cup syrup

*Put in your container and shake. No need to heat.*

## DAIRY FREE VERSION

Follow instructions above but use these substitutions:
- 1 can sweetened condensed coconut milk OR sweetened condensed oat milk
- 2 1/4 cups milk alternative of choice (or more as needed)

## EXPIRATION DATE

Use the expiration date listed on the milk or milk substitute that you used.

## NOTES

*Peanut Butter Cup Coffee Creamer*

*NUTRITIONAL FACTS: Homemade coffee creamer has less sugar, carbs, and calories than most store bought creamers. You can find nutritional fact calculators online to determine your exact nutritional facts based on the exact ingredients that you use. When comparing to store bought creamers, the recommended serving size is 1 tablespoon. This is the same serving size that store bought creamers recommend.*

# Peanut Butter Fluff

**CONTAINER SIZE:** 1 Quart (32 oz)

**MY RATING:** ☆☆☆☆☆

## INGREDIENTS

- 14 oz. sweetened condensed milk
- 2 tbsp. smooth peanut butter
- 2 cups milk of choice
- 1 tsp. vanilla extract
    - OR 1 tbsp. vanilla syrup
- 2-3 tbsp. marshmallow fluff
    - OR 4-5 tbsp. marshmallow flavored syrup

## DIRECTIONS

Combine all ingredients, mix well. Warm over medium heat for a few minutes until your mixture just starts to steam. Once it starts steaming, remove it from heat. Let it cool then transfer to your container.

## SUGAR FREE VERSION

- 3 cups milk of choice
- 3/4 cup sugar free peanut butter cup syrup
- 1/4 cup sugar free marshmallow syrup

*Put in your container and shake. No need to heat.*

## DAIRY FREE VERSION

Follow instructions above but use these substitutions:
- 1 can sweetened condensed coconut milk OR sweetened condensed oat milk
- 2 1/4 cups milk alternative of choice (or more as needed)

## EXPIRATION DATE

Use the expiration date listed on the milk or milk substitute that you used.

## NOTES

*Peanut Butter Fluff Coffee Creamer*

*NUTRITIONAL FACTS: Homemade coffee creamer has less sugar, carbs, and calories than most store bought creamers. You can find nutritional fact calculators online to determine your exact nutritional facts based on the exact ingredients that you use. When comparing to store bought creamers, the recommended serving size is 1 tablespoon. This is the same serving size that store bought creamers recommend.*

**CONTAINER SIZE: 1 Quart (32 oz)**

**MY RATING:** ☆☆☆☆☆

## INGREDIENTS

- 14 oz. sweetened condensed milk
- 2 cups coconut milk or milk of choice
- 1/2 cup pineapple juice
- 1 tsp. vanilla extract
    - OR 1 tbsp. vanilla syrup
- 2 tsp. coconut extract
    - OR 2 tbsp. coconut syrup
- OPTIONAL: 1-2 tsp. rum extract

## DIRECTIONS

Combine all ingredients, mix well. Warm over medium heat for a few minutes until your mixture just starts to steam. Once it starts steaming, remove it from heat. Let it cool then transfer to your container.

## SUGAR FREE VERSION

- 3 cups milk of choice
- 3/4 cup sugar free coconut syrup
- 1/4 cup sugar free pineapple syrup

*Put in your container and shake. No need to heat.*

## DAIRY FREE VERSION

Follow instructions above but use these substitutions:
- 1 can sweetened condensed coconut milk
- 2 1/4 cups of coconut milk

## EXPIRATION DATE

Use the expiration date listed on the milk or milk substitute that you used.

## NOTES

*Pina Colada Coffee Creamer*

*NUTRITIONAL FACTS: Homemade coffee creamer has less sugar, carbs, and calories than most store bought creamers. You can find nutritional fact calculators online to determine your exact nutritional facts based on the exact ingredients that you use. When comparing to store bought creamers, the recommended serving size is 1 tablespoon. This is the same serving size that store bought creamers recommend.*

**CONTAINER SIZE:** 1 Quart (32 oz)                    **MY RATING:** ☆☆☆☆☆

## INGREDIENTS

- 14 oz. sweetened condensed milk
- 2 cups milk of choice
- 1 tsp. vanilla extract
  - OR 1 tbsp. vanilla syrup
- 1 tsp. strawberry emulsion or extract
  - OR 4-5 tbsp. strawberry syrup
- 1 tbsp. powdered sugar

## DIRECTIONS

Combine all ingredients and mix well. Warm over medium heat for a few minutes until your mixture just starts to steam. Once it starts steaming, remove it from heat. Let it cool then transfer to your container.

## SUGAR FREE VERSION

- 3 cups milk of choice
- 1 cup sugar free strawberry syrup

*Put in your container and shake. No need to heat.*

## DAIRY FREE VERSION

Follow instructions above but use these substitutions:
- 1 can sweetened condensed coconut milk OR sweetened condensed oat milk
- 2 1/4 cups milk alternative of choice (or more as needed)

## EXPIRATION DATE

Use the expiration date listed on the milk or milk substitute that you used.

## NOTES

*Pink Frosting Coffee Creamer*

*NUTRITIONAL FACTS: Homemade coffee creamer has less sugar, carbs, and calories than most store bought creamers. You can find nutritional fact calculators online to determine your exact nutritional facts based on the exact ingredients that you use. When comparing to store bought creamers, the recommended serving size is 1 tablespoon. This is the same serving size that store bought creamers recommend.*

**Pistachio Latte**

**CONTAINER SIZE:** 1 Quart (32 oz)

**MY RATING:** ☆☆☆☆☆

## INGREDIENTS

- 14 oz. sweetened condensed milk
- 2 cups milk of choice
- 1 tsp. vanilla extract
    - OR 1 tbsp. vanilla syrup
- 1 tsp. pistachio emulsion
    - OR 4-5 tbsp. pistachio syrup
- 1 tsp. espresso powder

## DIRECTIONS

Combine sweetened condensed milk and espresso powder first. Mix well them add in all other ingredients. Warm over medium heat for a few minutes until your mixture just starts to steam. Once it starts steaming, remove it from heat. Let it cool then transfer to your container.

## SUGAR FREE VERSION

- 3 cups milk of choice
- 1 tsp. espresso powder
- 1 cup sugar free pistachio syrup

*Put in your container and shake. No need to heat.*

## DAIRY FREE VERSION

Follow instructions above but use these substitutions:
- 1 can sweetened condensed coconut milk OR sweetened condensed oat milk
- 2 1/4 cups milk alternative of choice (or more as needed)

## EXPIRATION DATE

Use the expiration date listed on the milk or milk substitute that you used.

## NOTES

*Pistachio Latte Coffee Creamer*

NUTRITIONAL FACTS: *Homemade coffee creamer has less sugar, carbs, and calories than most store bought creamers. You can find nutritional fact calculators online to determine your exact nutritional facts based on the exact ingredients that you use. When comparing to store bought creamers, the recommended serving size is 1 tablespoon. This is the same serving size that store bought creamers recommend.*

**CONTAINER SIZE:** 1 Quart (32 oz)

**MY RATING:** ☆ ☆ ☆ ☆ ☆

## INGREDIENTS

- 14 oz. sweetened condensed milk
- 2 cups milk of choice
- 2 tbsp. pumpkin puree
  *Pro-tip: freeze leftover pumpkin puree in 2 tbsp. cubes for quick use for your next batch of creamer*
- 2 tbsp. pure maple syrup
- 1 tsp. pumpkin pie spice
  - OR a pinch of ground ginger, cinnamon, nutmeg, cloves & allspice
- 1/4 tsp ground cinnamon

## DIRECTIONS

Combine sweetened condensed milk with all ground spices. Mix well then mix in all other ingredients. Warm over medium heat for a few minutes until your mixture just starts to steam. Once it starts steaming, remove it from heat. Let it cool then transfer to your container.

*It is normal for ground spices to settle during storage. Just give it a quick shake before each use. If you prefer no settling spices, you can strain your mixture through a cheesecloth to filter out the spices as you put it in your container.*

## SUGAR FREE VERSION

- 3 cups milk of choice
- 1 cup sugar free pumpkin spice syrup

*Put in your container and shake. No need to heat.*

## DAIRY FREE VERSION

Follow instructions above but use these substitutions:
- 1 can sweetened condensed coconut milk OR sweetened condensed oat milk
- 2 1/4 cups milk alternative of choice (or more as needed)

## EXPIRATION DATE

Use the expiration date listed on the milk or milk substitute that you used.

## NOTES

*Pumpkin Spice Coffee Creamer*

*NUTRITIONAL FACTS: Homemade coffee creamer has less sugar, carbs, and calories than most store bought creamers. You can find nutritional fact calculators online to determine your exact nutritional facts based on the exact ingredients that you use. When comparing to store bought creamers, the recommended serving size is 1 tablespoon. This is the same serving size that store bought creamers recommend.*

**CONTAINER SIZE:** 1 Quart (32 oz)

**MY RATING:** ☆☆☆☆☆

## INGREDIENTS

- 14 oz. sweetened condensed milk
- 2 cups milk of choice
- 2 tsp. vanilla extract
  - OR 2 tbsp. vanilla syrup
- 1 –2 tsp. red velvet emulsion
  - OR 4-5 tbsp. red velvet syrup
- 1 tsp. cream cheese emulsion
  - OR 1 tbsp. cream cheese

## DIRECTIONS

Combine all ingredients and mix well. Warm over medium heat for a few minutes until your mixture just starts to steam. Once it starts steaming, remove it from heat. Let it cool then transfer to your container.

## SUGAR FREE VERSION

- 3 cups milk of choice
- 1 cup sugar free red velvet syrup

*Put in your container and shake. No need to heat.*

## DAIRY FREE VERSION

Follow instructions above but use these substitutions:

- 1 can sweetened condensed coconut milk OR sweetened condensed oat milk
- 2 1/4 cups milk alternative of choice (or more as needed)

## EXPIRATION DATE

Use the expiration date listed on the milk or milk substitute that you used.

## NOTES

*Red Velvet Coffee Creamer*

*NUTRITIONAL FACTS: Homemade coffee creamer has less sugar, carbs, and calories than most store bought creamers. You can find nutritional fact calculators online to determine your exact nutritional facts based on the exact ingredients that you use. When comparing to store bought creamers, the recommended serving size is 1 tablespoon. This is the same serving size that store bought creamers recommend.*

# S'mores Creamer

**CONTAINER SIZE:** 1 Quart (32 oz)

**MY RATING:** ☆☆☆☆☆

## INGREDIENTS

- 14 oz. sweetened condensed milk
- 2 cups milk of choice
- 2 tbsp. unsweetened cocoa powder
  - OR 4 tbsp. mocha syrup
- 1 tsp. vanilla extract
  - OR 1 tbsp. vanilla syrup
- 3 tbsp. marshmallow fluff
  - OR 1/4 cup mini marshmallows
- 1/4 tsp. ground cinnamon *(optional)*
  - OR 1/4 tsp. cinnamon extract

## DIRECTIONS

Combine sweetened condensed milk, marshmallow fluff and cocoa powder first. Mix well then mix in all other ingredients. Warm over medium heat for a few minutes until your mixture just starts to steam. Once it starts steaming, remove it from heat. Let it cool then transfer to your container.

*It is normal for ground spices to settle during storage. Just give it a quick shake before each use. If you prefer no settling spices, you can strain your mixture through a cheesecloth to filter out the spices as you put it in your container.*

## SUGAR FREE VERSION

- 3 cups milk of choice
- 1 cup sugar free S'mores syrup

*Put in your container and shake. No need to heat.*

## DAIRY FREE VERSION

Follow instructions above but use these substitutions:
- 1 can sweetened condensed coconut milk OR sweetened condensed oat milk
- 2 1/4 cups milk alternative of choice (or more as needed)

## EXPIRATION DATE

Use the expiration date listed on the milk or milk substitute that you used.

## NOTES

S'mores Coffee Creamer

*NUTRITIONAL FACTS: Homemade coffee creamer has less sugar, carbs, and calories than most store bought creamers. You can find nutritional fact calculators online to determine your exact nutritional facts based on the exact ingredients that you use. When comparing to store bought creamers, the recommended serving size is 1 tablespoon. This is the same serving size that store bought creamers recommend.*

# Salted Caramel Mocha

**CONTAINER SIZE:**
1 Quart (32 oz)

**MY RATING:** ☆☆☆☆☆

## INGREDIENTS

- 14 oz. sweetened condensed milk
- 2 cups milk of choice
- 2- 4 tbsp. unsweetened cocoa powder
  - OR 1/4 cup–1/2 cup mocha syrup
- 1/4 cup caramel syrup or sauce
- 1 tsp. vanilla extract
  - OR 1 tbsp. vanilla syrup
- 1 tsp. sea salt

## DIRECTIONS

Combine sweetened condensed milk salt, and cocoa powder first. Mix well then mix in all other ingredients. Warm over medium heat for a few minutes until your mixture just starts to steam. Once it starts steaming, remove it from heat. Let it cool then transfer to your container.

*It is normal for ground spices to settle during storage. Just give it a quick shake before each use. If you prefer no settling spices, you can strain your mixture through a cheesecloth to filter out the spices as you put it in your container.*

## SUGAR FREE VERSION

- 3 cups milk of choice
- 1/2 cup sugar free salted caramel syrup
- 1/2 cup sugar free mocha syrup

*Put in your container and shake. No need to heat.*

## DAIRY FREE VERSION

Follow instructions above but use these substitutions:
- 1 can sweetened condensed coconut milk OR sweetened condensed oat milk
- 2 1/4 cups milk alternative of choice (or more as needed)

## EXPIRATION DATE

Use the expiration date listed on the milk or milk substitute that you used.

## NOTES

*Salted Caramel Mocha Coffee Creamer*

*NUTRITIONAL FACTS: Homemade coffee creamer has less sugar, carbs, and calories than most store bought creamers. You can find nutritional fact calculators online to determine your exact nutritional facts based on the exact ingredients that you use. When comparing to store bought creamers, the recommended serving size is 1 tablespoon. This is the same serving size that store bought creamers recommend.*

**CONTAINER SIZE:** 1 Quart (32 oz)

**MY RATING:** ☆☆☆☆☆

## INGREDIENTS

- 14 oz. sweetened condensed milk
- 2 cups milk of choice
- 1 tsp. vanilla extract
    - OR 1 tbsp. vanilla syrup
- 1/3 cup caramel sauce or syrup
- 1/2–1 tsp. sea salt

## DIRECTIONS

Combine all ingredients, mix well. Warm over medium heat for a few minutes until your mixture just starts to steam. Once it starts steaming, remove it from heat. Let it cool then transfer to your container.

## SUGAR FREE VERSION

- 3 cups milk of choice
- 1 cup sugar free salted caramel syrup

*Put in your container and shake. No need to heat.*

## DAIRY FREE VERSION

Follow instructions above but use these substitutions:
- 1 can sweetened condensed coconut milk OR sweetened condensed oat milk
- 2 1/4 cups milk alternative of choice (or more as needed)

## EXPIRATION DATE

Use the expiration date listed on the milk or milk substitute that you used.

## NOTES

*Salted Caramel Coffee Creamer*

*NUTRITIONAL FACTS: Homemade coffee creamer has less sugar, carbs, and calories than most store bought creamers. You can find nutritional fact calculators online to determine your exact nutritional facts based on the exact ingredients that you use. When comparing to store bought creamers, the recommended serving size is 1 tablespoon. This is the same serving size that store bought creamers recommend.*

# Snickerdoodle Creamer

**CONTAINER SIZE:** 1 Quart (32 oz)

**MY RATING:** ☆☆☆☆☆

*"Popular Cookie Flavor"*

## INGREDIENTS

- 14 oz. sweetened condensed milk
- 2 cups milk of choice
- 2 tsp. hazelnut bakery emulsion
    - OR 4 tbsp. hazelnut syrup
- 1 tbsp. vanilla extract
    - OR 3 tbsp. vanilla syrup
- 1 tsp. ground cinnamon
    - OR 1 tsp. cinnamon extract

## DIRECTIONS

Combine sweetened condensed milk and cinnamon first. Mix well then mix in all other ingredients. Warm over medium heat for a few minutes until your mixture just starts to steam. Once it starts steaming, remove it from heat. Let it cool then transfer to your container.

*It is normal for ground spices to settle during storage. Just give it a quick shake before each use. If you prefer no settling spices, you can strain your mixture through a cheesecloth to filter out the spices as you put it in your container.*

## SUGAR FREE VERSION

- 3 cups milk of choice
- 1/2 cup sugar free brown sugar cinnamon syrup
- 1/4 cup sugar free vanilla syrup
- 1/4 cup sugar free hazelnut syrup

*Put in your container and shake. No need to heat.*

## DAIRY FREE VERSION

Follow instructions above but use these substitutions:

- 1 can sweetened condensed coconut milk OR sweetened condensed oat milk
- 2 1/4 cups milk alternative of choice (or more as needed)

## EXPIRATION DATE

Use the expiration date listed on the milk or milk substitute that you used.

## NOTES

*Snickerdoodle Coffee Creamer*

**NUTRITIONAL FACTS:** Homemade coffee creamer has less sugar, carbs, and calories than most store bought creamers. You can find nutritional fact calculators online to determine your exact nutritional facts based on the exact ingredients that you use. When comparing to store bought creamers, the recommended serving size is 1 tablespoon. This is the same serving size that store bought creamers recommend.

**CONTAINER SIZE: 1 Quart (32 oz)**

**MY RATING:** ☆☆☆☆☆

## INGREDIENTS

- 1/4 cup pecans + 1 cup thin milk (blended)
- 14 oz. sweetened condensed milk
- 1 cup milk of choice
- 2 tsp. vanilla extract
  - OR 2 tbsp. vanilla syrup
- 2 tsp. butter extract
  - OR 1 tbsp butter
- Drizzle of caramel

## DIRECTIONS

Blend 1/4 cup pecans and 1 cup of 2% milk together until well blended. Using a fine mesh strainer, strain the pecan milk mixture as you pour it into the pan. Add in the rest of the ingredients. Warm over medium heat for a few minutes until your mixture just starts to steam. Once it starts steaming, remove it from heat. Let it cool then transfer to your container.

*The heating process allows the alcohol from the extracts to evaporate leaving you with a smoother tasting creamer. It also allows the ingredients to mix better. Do NOT let it boil. You should be able to stick your finger in without burning yourself.*

## SUGAR FREE VERSION

- 3 cups milk of choice
- 1 cup sugar free southern butter pecan syrup

*Put in your container and shake. No need to heat.*

## DAIRY FREE VERSION

Follow instructions above but use these substitutions:
- 1 can sweetened condensed coconut milk OR sweetened condensed oat milk
- 2 1/4 cups milk alternative of choice (or more as needed)

## EXPIRATION DATE

Use the expiration date listed on the milk or milk substitute that you used.

## NOTES

*Southern Butter Pecan Coffee Creamer*

*NUTRITIONAL FACTS: Homemade coffee creamer has less sugar, carbs, and calories than most store bought creamers. You can find nutritional fact calculators online to determine your exact nutritional facts based on the exact ingredients that you use. When comparing to store bought creamers, the recommended serving size is 1 tablespoon. This is the same serving size that store bought creamers recommend.*

# Strawberries & Cream

**CONTAINER SIZE:** 1 Quart (32 oz)

**MY RATING:** ☆ ☆ ☆ ☆ ☆

## INGREDIENTS

- 14 oz. sweetened condensed milk
- 2 cups milk of choice
- 1 tsp. vanilla extract
  - OR 1 tbsp. vanilla syrup
- 2 tsp. strawberry extract
  - OR 2 tbsp. strawberry syrup
- 1 tbsp. cream cheese
  - OR 1 tsp. cream cheese emulsion

## DIRECTIONS

Combine all ingredients, mix well. Warm over medium heat for a few minutes until your mixture just starts to steam. Once it starts steaming, remove it from heat. Let it cool then transfer to your container.

## SUGAR FREE VERSION

- 3 cups milk of choice
- 1 cup sugar free strawberry syrup
- 1 tsp. cream cheese emulsion

*Put in your container and shake. No need to heat.*

## DAIRY FREE VERSION

Follow instructions above but use these substitutions:
- 1 can sweetened condensed coconut milk OR sweetened condensed oat milk
- 2 1/4 cups milk alternative of choice (or more as needed)

## EXPIRATION DATE

Use the expiration date listed on the milk or milk substitute that you used.

## NOTES

*Strawberries & Cream Coffee Creamer*

*NUTRITIONAL FACTS: Homemade coffee creamer has less sugar, carbs, and calories than most store bought creamers. You can find nutritional fact calculators online to determine your exact nutritional facts based on the exact ingredients that you use. When comparing to store bought creamers, the recommended serving size is 1 tablespoon. This is the same serving size that store bought creamers recommend.*

**CONTAINER SIZE:** 1 Quart (32 oz)　　　　　　　　**MY RATING:** ☆☆☆☆☆

## INGREDIENTS

- 14 oz. sweetened condensed milk
- 2 cups rice milk
- 1 tsp. vanilla extract
  - OR 1 tbsp. vanilla syrup
- 1 tsp. strawberry extract
  - OR 2 tbsp. strawberry syrup
- 1 tbsp. brown sugar

## DIRECTIONS

Combine all ingredients, mix well. Warm over medium heat for a few minutes until your mixture just starts to steam. Once it starts steaming, remove it from heat. Let it cool then transfer to your container.

## SUGAR FREE VERSION

- 3 cups milk of choice
- 3/4 cup sugar free horchata syrup
- 1/4 cup sugar free strawberry syrup

*Put in your container and shake. No need to heat.*

## DAIRY FREE VERSION

Follow instructions above but use these substitutions:
- 1 can sweetened condensed coconut milk OR sweetened condensed oat milk
- 2 1/4 cups milk alternative of choice (or more as needed)

## EXPIRATION DATE

Use the expiration date listed on the milk or milk substitute that you used.

## NOTES

*Strawberry Horchata Coffee Creamer*

*NUTRITIONAL FACTS: Homemade coffee creamer has less sugar, carbs, and calories than most store bought creamers. You can find nutritional fact calculators online to determine your exact nutritional facts based on the exact ingredients that you use. When comparing to store bought creamers, the recommended serving size is 1 tablespoon. This is the same serving size that store bought creamers recommend.*

**Sugar Cookie**

**CONTAINER SIZE:** 1 Quart (32 oz)

**MY RATING:** ☆☆☆☆☆

*"Popular Cookie Flavor"*

## INGREDIENTS

- 14 oz. sweetened condensed milk
- 2 cups milk of choice
- 2 tsp. vanilla extract
    - OR 2 tbsp. vanilla syrup
- 1/2 tsp. almond extract
    - OR 1/2 tsp. almond emulsion
- 1 tbsp. powdered sugar

## DIRECTIONS

Combine all ingredients, mix well. Warm over medium heat for a few minutes until your mixture just starts to steam. Once it starts steaming, remove it from heat. Let it cool then transfer to your container.

## SUGAR FREE VERSION

- 3 cups milk of choice
- 1 cup sugar free sugar cookie syrup

*Put in your container and shake. No need to heat.*

## DAIRY FREE VERSION

Follow instructions above but use these substitutions:

- 1 can sweetened condensed coconut milk OR sweetened condensed oat milk
- 2 1/4 cups milk alternative of choice (or more as needed)

## EXPIRATION DATE

Use the expiration date listed on the milk or milk substitute that you used.

## NOTES

*Sugar Cookie Coffee Creamer*

**NUTRITIONAL FACTS:** Homemade coffee creamer has less sugar, carbs, and calories than most store bought creamers. You can find nutritional fact calculators online to determine your exact nutritional facts based on the exact ingredients that you use. When comparing to store bought creamers, the recommended serving size is 1 tablespoon. This is the same serving size that store bought creamers recommend.

# Sweet Cream

**CONTAINER SIZE:** 1 Quart (32 oz)

**MY RATING:** ☆☆☆☆☆

## INGREDIENTS

- 14 oz. sweetened condensed milk
- 2 cups milk of choice
- 1 tsp. vanilla extract

*NOTE: Make ANY flavor of coffee creamer you want with this base recipe by adding 4-5 tbsp. flavored syrup of your choice OR 1-2 tsp of any extract of choice. The flavor possibilities are truly endless!*

## DIRECTIONS

Combine all ingredients and mix well. Warm over medium heat for a few minutes until your mixture just starts to steam. Once it starts steaming, remove it from heat. Let it cool then transfer to your container.

## SUGAR FREE VERSION

- 3 cups milk of choice
- 1 cup sugar free simple syrup

*Put in your container and shake. No need to heat.*

## DAIRY FREE VERSION

Follow instructions above but use these substitutions:

- 1 can sweetened condensed coconut milk OR sweetened condensed oat milk
- 2 1/4 cups milk alternative of choice (or more as needed)

## EXPIRATION DATE

Use the expiration date listed on the milk or milk substitute that you used.

## NOTES

*Basic Sweet Cream*

*NUTRITIONAL FACTS: Homemade coffee creamer has less sugar, carbs, and calories than most store bought creamers. You can find nutritional fact calculators online to determine your exact nutritional facts based on the exact ingredients that you use. When comparing to store bought creamers, the recommended serving size is 1 tablespoon. This is the same serving size that store bought creamers recommend.*

# Sweetened Condensed Milk

**CONTAINER SIZE:** 1.5 cup container

**MY RATING:** ☆☆☆☆☆

## INGREDIENTS

- 2 cups whole milk
- 3/4 cup sugar, honey or sweetener of choice
- 1/4 cup salted butter
- 1 tsp. vanilla extract

## DIRECTIONS

Whisk together milk and sweetener in a medium saucepan over medium-low heat. Whisking often, bring to a low simmer. Continue to simmer, whisking often, until milk has reduced by half, about 30 minutes. DO NOT COVER. Once reduced, remove from heat and stir in butter and vanilla. Mixture will thicken more as it cools.

## SUGAR FREE VERSION

- 2 1/2 cups heavy cream
- 3/4 cup sugar alternative
  - Monk fruit sweetener, erythritol, allulose, or sugar free brown sugar, etc.
- 1/4 cup salted butter
- 1 tsp. vanilla extract

*Once it begins to simmer, reduce the heat to very low. Let the condensed milk simmer for around 45 minutes.*

## DAIRY FREE VERSION

- 1 (14 oz.) can lite canned coconut milk
- ½ cup sugar or sweetener of choice
- 1 tsp. vanilla extract
- 1/4 tsp. salt
- 1/2 cup unsweetened plain dairy-free milk beverage (preferably thicker one)

*Once it begins to simmer, reduce the heat to very low. Let the condensed milk simmer for around 25 minutes.*

## EXPIRATION DATE

Lasts 7-10 days in the refrigerator.

## NOTES

**CONTAINER SIZE:** 1 Quart (32 oz)

**MY RATING:** ☆☆☆☆☆

*"Nutty Caramel"*

## INGREDIENTS

- 14 oz. sweetened condensed milk
- 2 cups milk of choice
- 1 tsp. vanilla extract
    - OR 1 tbsp. vanilla syrup
- 3 tbsp. caramel sauce or syrup
- 2 tsp. almond extract
    - OR 2 tbsp. almond syrup

## DIRECTIONS

Combine all ingredients, mix well. Warm over medium heat for a few minutes until your mixture just starts to steam. Once it starts steaming, remove it from heat. Let it cool then transfer to your container.

## SUGAR FREE VERSION

- 3 cups milk of choice
- 1 cup sugar free Toffee Nut syrup

*Put in your container and shake. No need to heat.*

## DAIRY FREE VERSION

Follow instructions above but use these substitutions:
- 1 can sweetened condensed coconut milk OR sweetened condensed oat milk
- 2 1/4 cups milk alternative of choice (or more as needed)

## EXPIRATION DATE

Use the expiration date listed on the milk or milk substitute that you used.

## NOTES

*Toffee Nut Coffee Creamer*

*NUTRITIONAL FACTS: Homemade coffee creamer has less sugar, carbs, and calories than most store bought creamers. You can find nutritional fact calculators online to determine your exact nutritional facts based on the exact ingredients that you use. When comparing to store bought creamers, the recommended serving size is 1 tablespoon. This is the same serving size that store bought creamers recommend.*

**CONTAINER SIZE:** 1 Quart (32 oz)

**MY RATING:** ☆ ☆ ☆ ☆ ☆

## INGREDIENTS

- 14 oz. sweetened condensed milk
- 2 cups milk of choice
- 2 tsp. vanilla extract
    - OR 2 tbsp. vanilla syrup
- 2 tsp. buttery sweet dough emulsion
- 1 tsp. cream cheese emulsion
    - OR 1 tbsp. cream cheese

## DIRECTIONS

Combine all ingredients and mix well. Warm over medium heat for a few minutes until your mixture just starts to steam. Once it starts steaming, remove it from heat. Let it cool then transfer to your container.

## SUGAR FREE VERSION

- 3 cups milk of choice
- 1 cup sugar free vanilla cannoli syrup
    - OR 1 cup sugar free vanilla syrup
    - + 1 tsp. cream cheese emulsion

*Put in your container and shake. No need to heat.*

## DAIRY FREE VERSION

Follow instructions above but use these substitutions:
- 1 can sweetened condensed coconut milk OR sweetened condensed oat milk
- 2 1/4 cups milk alternative of choice (or more as needed)

## EXPIRATION DATE

Use the expiration date listed on the milk or milk substitute that you used.

## NOTES

*Vanilla Cannoli Coffee Creamer*

*NUTRITIONAL FACTS: Homemade coffee creamer has less sugar, carbs, and calories than most store bought creamers. You can find nutritional fact calculators online to determine your exact nutritional facts based on the exact ingredients that you use. When comparing to store bought creamers, the recommended serving size is 1 tablespoon. This is the same serving size that store bought creamers recommend.*

# Vanilla Caramel

**CONTAINER SIZE:** 1 Quart (32 oz)

**MY RATING:** ☆☆☆☆☆

## INGREDIENTS

- 14 oz. sweetened condensed milk
- 2 cups milk of choice
- 1 tbsp. vanilla extract
    - OR 4 tbsp. vanilla syrup
- 1/4 cup caramel sauce or syrup of choice

## DIRECTIONS

Combine all ingredients and mix well. Warm over medium heat for a few minutes until your mixture just starts to steam. Once it starts steaming, remove it from heat. Let it cool then transfer to your container.

## SUGAR FREE VERSION

- 3 cups milk of choice
- 1/2 cup sugar free caramel syrup
- 1/2 cup sugar free vanilla syrup

*Put in your container and shake. No need to heat.*

## DAIRY FREE VERSION

Follow instructions above but use these substitutions:
- 1 can sweetened condensed coconut milk OR sweetened condensed oat milk
- 2 1/4 cups milk alternative of choice (or more as needed)

## EXPIRATION DATE

Use the expiration date listed on the milk or milk substitute that you used.

## NOTES

*Vanilla Caramel Coffee Creamer*

*NUTRITIONAL FACTS: Homemade coffee creamer has less sugar, carbs, and calories than most store bought creamers. You can find nutritional fact calculators online to determine your exact nutritional facts based on the exact ingredients that you use. When comparing to store bought creamers, the recommended serving size is 1 tablespoon. This is the same serving size that store bought creamers recommend.*

# Vanilla Creamer

**CONTAINER SIZE:** 1 Quart (32 oz)

**MY RATING:** ☆☆☆☆☆

## INGREDIENTS

- 14 oz. sweetened condensed milk
- 2 cups milk of choice
- 1 tbsp. vanilla extract or vanilla bean paste
    - OR 4-5 tbsp. vanilla syrup

## DIRECTIONS

Combine all ingredients and mix well. Warm over medium heat for a few minutes until your mixture just starts to steam. Once it starts steaming, remove it from heat. Let it cool then transfer to your container.

## SUGAR FREE VERSION

- 3 cups milk of choice
- 1 cup sugar free vanilla syrup

*Put in your container and shake. No need to heat.*

## DAIRY FREE VERSION

Follow instructions above but use these substitutions:
- 1 can sweetened condensed coconut milk OR sweetened condensed oat milk
- 2 1/4 cups milk alternative of choice (or more as needed)

## EXPIRATION DATE

Use the expiration date listed on the milk or milk substitute that you used.

## NOTES

Vanilla Coffee Creamer

**NUTRITIONAL FACTS:** Homemade coffee creamer has less sugar, carbs, and calories than most store bought creamers. You can find nutritional fact calculators online to determine your exact nutritional facts based on the exact ingredients that you use. When comparing to store bought creamers, the recommended serving size is 1 tablespoon. This is the same serving size that store bought creamers recommend.

**CONTAINER SIZE:**
1 Quart (32 oz)

**MY RATING:** ☆ ☆ ☆ ☆ ☆

## INGREDIENTS

- 14 oz. sweetened condensed milk
- 2 cups milk of choice
- 1 tsp. vanilla extract
  - OR 1 tbsp. vanilla syrup
- 3 tbsp. white cocoa powder
  - OR 1/3 cup white chocolate chips
- 1 tsp. espresso powder

## DIRECTIONS

Combine sweetened condensed milk and cocoa powder first. Mix well then mix in all other ingredients. Warm over medium heat for a few minutes until your mixture just starts to steam. Once it starts steaming, remove it from heat. Let it cool then transfer to your container.

## SUGAR FREE VERSION

- 3 cups milk of choice
- 1 cup sugar free white chocolate mocha syrup

*Put in your container and shake. No need to heat.*

## DAIRY FREE VERSION

Follow instructions above but use these substitutions:
- 1 can sweetened condensed coconut milk OR sweetened condensed oat milk
- 2 1/4 cups milk alternative of choice (or more as needed)

## EXPIRATION DATE

Use the expiration date listed on the milk or milk substitute that you used.

## NOTES

*White Chocolate Mocha Coffee Creamer*

*NUTRITIONAL FACTS: Homemade coffee creamer has less sugar, carbs, and calories than most store bought creamers. You can find nutritional fact calculators online to determine your exact nutritional facts based on the exact ingredients that you use. When comparing to store bought creamers, the recommended serving size is 1 tablespoon. This is the same serving size that store bought creamers recommend.*

# White Chocolate Raspberry

**CONTAINER SIZE:** 1 Quart (32 oz)

**MY RATING:** ☆☆☆☆☆

## INGREDIENTS

- 14 oz. sweetened condensed milk
- 2 cups milk of choice
- 2 tbsp. raspberry syrup
    - OR 1 tsp. raspberry bakery emulsion
- 4 tbsp. white chocolate syrup
    - OR 1/3 cup white chocolate chips

## DIRECTIONS

Combine all ingredients, mix well. Warm over medium heat for a few minutes until your mixture just starts to steam. Once it starts steaming, remove it from heat. Let it cool then transfer to your container.

## SUGAR FREE VERSION

- 3 cups milk of choice
- 3/4 cup sugar free white chocolate syrup
- 1/4 cup sugar free raspberry syrup

*Put in your container and shake. No need to heat.*

## DAIRY FREE VERSION

Follow instructions above but use these substitutions:
- 1 can sweetened condensed coconut milk OR sweetened condensed oat milk
- 2 1/4 cups milk alternative of choice (or more as needed)

## EXPIRATION DATE

Use the expiration date listed on the milk or milk substitute that you used.

## NOTES

*White Chocolate Raspberry Coffee Creamer*

*NUTRITIONAL FACTS: Homemade coffee creamer has less sugar, carbs, and calories than most store bought creamers. You can find nutritional fact calculators online to determine your exact nutritional facts based on the exact ingredients that you use. When comparing to store bought creamers, the recommended serving size is 1 tablespoon. This is the same serving size that store bought creamers recommend.*

**CONTAINER SIZE:**

**MY RATING:** ☆☆☆☆☆

## INGREDIENTS

## DIRECTIONS

## EXPIRATION DATE

## NOTES

**CONTAINER SIZE:**

**MY RATING:** ☆☆☆☆☆

## INGREDIENTS

## DIRECTIONS

## EXPIRATION DATE

## NOTES

# My Own Recipe

**CONTAINER SIZE:**

**MY RATING:** ☆☆☆☆☆

## INGREDIENTS

## DIRECTIONS

## EXPIRATION DATE

## NOTES

# My Own Recipe

**CONTAINER SIZE:**

**MY RATING:** ☆☆☆☆☆

## INGREDIENTS

## DIRECTIONS

## EXPIRATION DATE

## NOTES

**CONTAINER SIZE:**

**MY RATING:** ☆☆☆☆☆

## INGREDIENTS

## DIRECTIONS

## EXPIRATION DATE

## NOTES

## My Own Recipe

**CONTAINER SIZE:**

**MY RATING:** ☆☆☆☆☆

### INGREDIENTS

### DIRECTIONS

### EXPIRATION DATE

### NOTES

# My Own Recipe

**CONTAINER SIZE:**

**MY RATING:** ☆☆☆☆☆

## INGREDIENTS

## DIRECTIONS

## EXPIRATION DATE

## NOTES

# My Own Recipe

**CONTAINER SIZE:**

**MY RATING:** ☆☆☆☆☆

## INGREDIENTS

## DIRECTIONS

## EXPIRATION DATE

## NOTES

# My Own Recipe

**CONTAINER SIZE:**

**MY RATING:** ☆☆☆☆☆

## INGREDIENTS

## DIRECTIONS

## EXPIRATION DATE

## NOTES

**CONTAINER SIZE:**

**MY RATING:** ☆☆☆☆☆

## INGREDIENTS

## DIRECTIONS

## EXPIRATION DATE

## NOTES

Made in United States
Troutdale, OR
11/11/2024

24619063R00052